Viva le Resistance!

The girls in our class are probably a lot like the girls in every eighth grade class. There are the pretty ones, the skinny ones, the athletic ones, the short ones, the tall ones, the mean cliquey ones, the loners…. you get the picture.

It's kind of hard to find the place to fit in. I am athletic, but not really the "jock" type. I'm not ugly, but definitely not one of the "the pretty ones."

The "*chosen ones.*"

Viva le Resistance!

Annie Books series by Michelle Fattig

www.anniebooks.com

A Windy Day with Annie

A Prairie Day with Annie

Bully-Be-Gone with Annie

Viva Le Resistance!

Coming soon to Annie Books

Making Friends and Keeping Them with Annie

Learning to be Nice with Annie

Stopping the Blurting Days with Annie

Managing the Distracto-Days with Annie

Calming the Stormy Days with Annie

Viva le Resistance!

www.anniebooks.com

by Michelle Fattig, Ed.S.

pictures by Josh Fattig

Annie Books©

Flower by the Water Publishing Genoa, NE

Viva le Resistance!

This book is dedicated
to my wonderful husband,
amazing children,
and our family.

Copyright © 2007 by Michelle Fattig.
All rights reserved under international and Pan American
Copyright Conventions. Published in the United States by Flower
by the Water Publishing.
Fattig, Michelle. *Viva le Resistance!* / Michelle Fattig ;
Illustrated by Josh Fattig. p. 218
"Annie Books" SUMMARY: In her own words, a young girl
describes her feelings and emotions about living with Attention
Deficit Disorder, bullies, peer pressure, making good choices and
'the cliquey's.'
ISBN 978-0-9795805-3-6(pbk)

Manufactured in the United States of America.

Viva le Resistance!

Prologue

Mom forgot to set the alarm last night. She raced into my room about five minutes ago yelling, "Get up! Get up! We are running late! You have less than twenty minutes before the bus starts honking!"

Twenty minutes!?

I can't be ready in TWENTY minutes!

It takes me TEN, just to get my eyes all of the way open!

"NOW kids!" she hollers down the stairs. I can hear her slamming around in the kitchen.

Viva le Resistance!

My brother and I simultaneously bark back, "We ARE up." Although neither of actually had gotten out of bed yet! We both have a bedroom in the basement.

With a groan, I roll out of bed and feel my feet hit the freakishly cold floor. Living in the basement means we have cement floors. Sure we have carpeting over the cement, but it does little to diminish the chill permeating my tootsies!

Cement floors, on warm feet in the morning, are NOT an enjoyable experience.

I dress in a flash, putting on my favorite pair of shorts and a simple white shirt. I throw on socks and....

Viva le Resistance!

"MOM!"

MO-O-OM!"

MOM! I can't find my shoe!" I bellow from my room in the basement.

Why is it, that whenever I am late for the bus, some vital piece of my wardrobe winds up missing?

Racing up the stairs and into the bathroom, I kick my morning routine into high gear, and hastily brush my teeth, brush my hair and pull it back into a haphazard ponytail. I wash my face, slap my cheeks, and bite my lips for color.

No time for makeup today!

Viva le Resistance!

My brother and sister are beating on the door.

"Hurry up!"

"Unlock the door!"

"It's my turn in there!"

We only have one bathroom.

"Come ON! WE have to get ready TOO!"

I wait a few moments, just to torture them, and then WHIP the door open, with a glare that says, "How DARE you rush my morning *toilette*!"

They shove their way in, knocking me to the side, where I encounter a towel rack in my ribs.

Viva le Resistance!

"Oooph!"

"Geez guys, act like a couple of animals, why don't you?" I mutter, as I head towards the kitchen.

Mom has foregone the usual cereal or bacon and eggs route, due to the time, or lack thereof, and instead chocolate chip cookies are sitting on the table, along with three glasses of milk.

Nice.

At my expression, mom shrugs and says with a hapless grin, "Hey. They have eggs and flour in them don't they?"

The woman has a point!

Viva le Resistance!

As I sit down to eat, my sister and brother barrel into the kitchen.

"Move!"

"Look out!"

"Mo-OM he hit me!"

"Did not!"

"Did too!"

"Did NOT!"

"KNOCK IT OFF!" I howl.

Mom rushed out the door, pulling her ratty, light blue robe closer around her waist, tossing out over her shoulder, "Kids, be nice and eat quickly."

I look outside, while putting my coat on, and grabbing my backpack.

Viva le Resistance!

Mom is standing at the end of our driveway, looking down the road in the direction the bus usually arrives. Her short, dark hair is whipping wildly around her face, and she is wearing her slippers along with the old robe.

Mom is bent forward slightly, as if bracing against the wind. Her right arm is wrapped tightly around her waist, trying in vain to hold the tattered material closed, while her left hand has the collar in a death grip under her chin, trying to afford some small amount of warmth.

Viva le Resistance!

She lets go with her left hand, and waves at the bus driver in a signal to wait, and that we are coming.

She lets go with her right hand, to wave us out more quickly.

Of course, her robe FLEW open, whipping wildly behind her.

My mother is now standing at the road with an ugly, ratty old robe thrashing out behind her, in her slippers AND pajamas, in front of all of my friends on the bus.

Of course, everyone on the bus has gotten out of their seats and moved to the windows lining the side, to get a better look.

Viva le Resistance!

Oh this day is just getting better and
better.

"Love you!" She yells, as we walk past her
and step up into the bus. Mom is now tugging
her robe back to some semblance of modesty.

Viva le Resistance!

"Yeah, love you too," I mutter inaudibly, completely mortified.

Viva le Resistance!

Chapter One

It's ten 'til eight.

Here we go again.

The bus is pulling up in front of the
school and, as usual, my stomach is in absolute
knots. Change in routine of any kind, even
those I am expecting, can be a pain.

If high school is supposed to be the best
years of your life, what is middle school
supposed to be?

My name is Annie. I am in eighth
grade, and I live on a farm outside of a small

Viva le Resistance!

town called Center City. I have something
called ADD, I call it A Distracto Disorder, but
everyone else calls it Attention Deficit
Disorder.

I moved around a lot when I was
younger and have gone to several schools.
This is actually the largest school that I've ever
attended. There are about 80 kids in my grade,
of which I am a friend with only a few. It can
be kind of a pain trying to make or keep
friends when you have ADD. Girls can be
hard to read, what with the smiling and
giggling, followed by the insults behind your
back. You kind of feel like you are walking on
eggshells when you try to fit in.

Viva le Resistance!

Boys are easier to read. If they are mad, they tell you. If they like you, well, they won't always tell you, but you can tell, you know?

The boys are pretty nice, but who wants to hang around with a bunch of guys who believe that making disgusting noises and nasty gestures under their desks in Algebra, when Mr. Nelson isn't looking, is a good time?

When I first started school here, we were in 6th grade. It was a tough year at best, what with the 'growing out before you grow up' situation going on.

You know what I mean?

All of the sudden, the normal, relatively average body you once knew, expands almost

3

before your eyes! My mom always told me I was just getting ready to grow and that everyone goes through it.

Why is it then that this "everybody" she speaks of appears to consist roughly of just me? Also, if this is so "normal," why is it that the doctor recommended a diet and she and my dad offered to bribe me to try it?

Does this "everybody" get offered $20.00 to cut back on the bread and butter too?

Normal?

Right!

I broke my foot in a weird accident and ended up on crutches for a few weeks that year. Paula was assigned to help me carry my books around and she seemed pretty nice. We actually began to become pretty good friends for a while.

We spent the night at each other's houses and generally got a long pretty well. Unfortunately, she developed a bizarre smell about her. I'm not sure what that was all about. Not something I thought would make for good conversation.

"Hey Paula. I noticed you have switched perfumes or something. Is the fragrance au de road kill?"

Maybe if I were a better friend, I could have found a way to gently suggest something. Being a sixth grader though, it just didn't work out. Needless to say, that friendship ended before it really had a chance.

Seventh grade was uneventful, except that I grew like seven inches over the summer and vaguely resembled Chewbacca in stature, compared to everyone else. I was actually about five inches taller than my brother, who is two years older than me.

For some reason, the growth spurt didn't solve the 'grown out before up' situation, and I actually blocked out the sun in certain circumstances.

Not really.

It just felt that way.

I've now settled into a comfortable 5'5."

Viva le Resistance!

Not too tall, not too short.

Eighth grade has been much more interesting. We are given a little more respect from the adults, but the homework is more tedious. Mr. Nelson, who I mentioned before with regard to the pervert guys in our class, is a pretty good guy. He supervises us at lunch and is kind of our honorary favorite teacher.

The only problem is, when he talks, there is a strange phenomenon that occurs. A stringy white substance starts at the corner of his mouth. As the class period progresses, it moves more towards the center of his lips and is very stringy. It stays there, stuck to his top and bottom lip, stretching as he talks.

Viva le Resistance!

Loooong…short……sideways
slightly….short….oooh ick….it almost flew
out at Robbie…loooong..short.

You get the picture.

It happens every day.

Everyone knows about it.

But no one knows what it is.

Viva le Resistance!

It probably would make a very good science project. Maybe even a ribbon winning science project.

It could have great impact on the scientific world, as we know it. But no one has the nerve to ask for his participation!

The girls in our class are probably a lot like the girls in every eighth grade class. There are the pretty ones, the skinny ones, the athletic ones, the short ones, the tall ones, the mean cliquey ones, the loners…. you get the picture.

It's kind of hard to find the place to fit in. I am athletic, but not really the "jock" type. I'm not ugly, but definitely not one of the "the pretty ones."

Viva le Resistance!

The "chosen ones."

The ones who walk around together and equally glare or cut down anyone they don't like. Which is pretty much anyone not walking around with them.

This, of course, does not correlate with how they treat the boys!

Is this a big shocker?

NOT!

The guys in our class fall into similar categories, with the addition of the stoners, geeks, and motor-heads. But there is one additional group, which may in fact be unique to our town.

Viva le Resistance!

They are…the bagmen. They aren't the type of bagmen you think about in general. Not the homeless kind.

These are "the guys."

They are THE main men. They are THE guys to know and be seen with. They carry "the" book bags. Not just any book bags. They carry THE same brand, size, shape, color, and logo.

These are the Cadillac of book bags.

They are the one, the only…The Phat Times 20, book bags.

The bagmen tried briefly to unify as well with jean jackets, Pe Pe jean jackets, but the look just didn't make it for them. I guess it was just too grease-lightnin' or something.

For another brief and not so shining moment, the bagmen also believed they were styling and profiling when they pilfered their dads' jeans as a new uniform. These were, of course, not just any jeans.

They had to be dad-sized pilfered Levi button-fly jeans.

After a few days of either being pants'ed by upperclassmen, or tripping over themselves as the jeans inevitably fell to their knees, they gave up on that particular fashion statement as well. The bagmen settled on, and ultimately became "the bagmen," when they adopted The Phat Times 20 book bags.

Sam and Lane are the unofficial and un-elected leaders. The bagmen officially consist of Sam, Lane, Tom, Keith, Ted, and Ron. The bagmen have a complicated hierarchy level, like most social entities.

Sam is tall, for an eighth grader. He has strawberry blond hair, braces, and freckles. He is probably average looking, but I find him utterly captivating! He is, of course, on the football team, basketball team, and track team.

He is yummy!

Lane is short.

Very short.

Very, very, very short.

He has blond hair that is cut very short. Like him, his hair is very, very, very short. He and Sam spend most waking moments together.

They walk alike, talk alike, and ..well…you get the picture.

They spend a lot of time talking in class. Teachers got so fed up with them, that they made them sit at opposite corners of the classroom one day. The next day Sam and Lane showed up with walkie-talkies, so they could still converse from across the classroom. The teachers gave up and let them sit together again.

Viva le Resistance!

Lane is also into athletics. He and Sam are both probably the best players on the teams.

Lane likes Laurie.

Laurie is my best and only true friend.

Tom is the heavy guy. He is the one who doesn't seem to have the "with it" look of the rest, but is somehow accepted anyway. Tom is going with Tori. She is the token heavy girl from the cliquey's. It's actually pretty cute to see them together.

They both have dark hair, cut to medium length. They are shaped roughly the same. When they walk together, holding hands, it makes you think of fraternal twins or something.

Tom and Tori...kind of makes you think of Jack and Jill doesn't it?

Keith is sort of the 'fringe' member. He fits in, but he's really a hanger-on part of the group. They accept him and his backpack, but he's new this year and so he's still kind of figuring out where he fits in the big scheme of things. Keith has really dark hair and eyes. His hair is really straight and hangs down over his eyes. He kind of reminds me of a lost puppy dog.

In a way, we look alike.

Viva le Resistance!

His hair and eyes are almost exactly the color of mine.

Ted and Ron are just Ted and Ron. They don't add a lot of flavor to the group, but they do provide the numbers. An in crowd can't really just consist of four people. It just wouldn't be quite so impressive. Ted has red hair and a lot of freckles. He is sort of the comic relief of the group.

Ron is the gorgeous one.

He is truly and remarkably amazing. It's almost like a light shines from behind him when walks into a room. He is tall and lanky. His hair is light brown with a golden highlight to it. His eyes are green with the longest, thickest eyelashes you've ever seen. Most of Ron's day is taken up with staring at himself in a mirror, window, or even the glass front of the fire extinguisher, if need be.

Ron is also not very bright.

He goes with Katie.

Katie is really cute, in a Scottish terrier sort of way. She is short and compact. Katie has sort of honey blond hair that is shoulder length, but is so coarse it doesn't really move. She has light colored eyes and a beautiful smile.

It's too bad that the smile is a fake, and she spends more time gossiping and cutting others down, than breathing, it seems. Of course she would NEVER let the boys see anything but the cute, bubbly side of her pseudo-personality.

Last month Katie got head lice.

It was one of the greatest days of my life.

She called a friend to confide.

Being that the friend was also a cliquey, and therefore a nasty gossip as well; her friend told a friend who told a friend and so on. Eventually the entire school knew her embarrassing secret.

Like I said, it was one of the greatest days of my life!

Viva le Resistance!

A couple of non-invited, non-preferred members tried to sidle into the group with a cheap knockoff of The Phat Times 20, one sad and scary day. It was as if a military infiltration of the pentagon was occurring.

It was mayhem I tell you!

It briefly shook the foundation of all that we know to be good and right about good old Center City Middle School.

Luckily, they were squelched and put firmly back in their place, OUTSIDE of THE group, quickly and quietly.

(Brief moment of quiet reflection needed.)

Whew.

Viva le Resistance!

Thanks, where was I?

Viva le Resistance!

Chapter Two

One day, I happened to be walking through the hallway at lunchtime. The bagmen were, of course, dining together. In a vulnerable moment, they had left their book bags unguarded, unsupervised, unaccounted for.

Unbelievable.

How could I pass up this chance of a lifetime? How could I turn away and walk on by? How could I just leave them alone and not mess with them just a little? How could I not respect the dignity of the position of bagman in this great school?

Oh come on.

Who could resist such utterly delightful temptation?

I quickly glanced to my left.

To my left, was a long hallway, with two entrances to the gym on one side, and several classroom doorways on the right. There was also an exit door at the end of the long hallway, right across from the band room doors.

All clear.

I glanced to my right. To my right were rows and rows of lockers, broken up only by intermittent classroom doorways.

Viva le Resistance!

Also clear.

Careful now.

Not too obvious.

Covertly, I look forward. In front of me
are two wide glass exit doors. Beyond the
doors, is a grassy area with benches.

Shoot!!

The cliquey's are milling about in their
usual herd of nastiness.

The really great thing about the
cliquey's, is that they are way too self absorbed
to notice anything outside the realm of THEM,
when they have, in their direct field of vision,
rows and rows and rows of windows to the
cafeteria. They are temporarily blinded and

entranced by visions of their own beauty reflected by the sterile wall of glass.

"I'm still okay," I was thinking.

Now, one final glance behind me reveals a long hallway. The main foyer of the school intersects this particular hallway. There is an atrium, rows of glass trophy cases, benches, and the main restrooms.

Clear.

With stealth, I quickly knelt to retrieve the precious book bags. They were placed neatly, lovingly together almost as if the bagmen had tucked them in for a nap.

Viva le Resistance!

I gathered The Phat Times 20 book bags gingerly, trying to be as absolutely nonchalant as possible.

I can't believe I am actually breaking out in a sweat!

There is literally a film of sweat on my upper lip.

This is going to be good.

With another glance in all directions, the cliquey's are still mesmerized by their beauty and, therefore, totally unaware of my subterfuge, I dart quickly towards the restrooms.

Almost there, almost there, almost…THERE!

Viva le Resistance!

Whew!

I'm in the clear.

Now what?

I looked for hiding place. Quick, quick...someone could see me at any second! Where, where...I look furtively around.

THERE!

The trash can!

It is the perfect hiding place.

In they go, quickly now.

Out, out, have to get out.... taking a seat...looking innocent...now, to sit back and watch the show!

Only a few minutes to the bell...should be interesting.

Viva le Resistance!

You'd think an abduction had taken place!

The place went into an uproar.

The bell rang.

Kids started meandering out of the double doors from the cafeteria. Some were laughing, others were talking, some were alone, and they just kept pouring out.

I waited with baited breath.

I didn't want to *look* like I was looking.

Oh, but the suspense!

Can you just FEEL it?

At first the bagmen strolled out as usual. The swaggers, the jostling, the goofing around, and then stunned silence ensued.

Viva le Resistance!

Sam and Lane were, of course, in front of the others. As they came to an abrupt halt, the others stumbled into them. The bagmen in back grumbled a bit.

It only took a moment for them all to stop and stare incredulously. Their mouths dropped open and their eyes bulged. No one could believe it. The precious bags were GONE!

Mayhem ensued.

The yelling, the running, the howls of despair and agony, I tell you it was awesome! This ranked right up there with they day I found out about Katie's head lice!

Viva le Resistance!

Then came the accusations. They
snatched up anyone and everyone around them
accusing, questioning, threatening.

"Who took our bags?" they yelled.

"Did you?"

"Was it you?"

"Not funny man."

"Really man, not funny at all."

It went on and on. As the bell rang, I
quietly strolled towards class.

"No need to ease their pain yet," I
thought to myself.

After they'd suffered sufficiently, I'd
just leave a note suggesting where to look. My
fun was spoiled, by a sixth grade girl, who

exited the bathroom with one lonely backpack held up in her hand and a confused look on her face.

She found the stash, and wondered why anyone was throwing away such nice backpacks!

Oh well. For a brief, but fleeting moment it had been great!

Chapter Three

Here we are.

It doesn't look all that intimidating.

It is just your everyday, average brick school building. But for some reason, just walking in makes me feel like throwing up. I have never noticed anyone else looking nauseous.

I guess it's just me.

"Hey Laurie. Did you get your Algebra done?" I asked.

"Yeah, it wasn't bad," she answered.

Viva le Resistance!

Laurie is the resident genius girl in our class. We went to a small country school together when we were younger. Laurie and I live on farms that are only about a mile from each other. Laurie and her cousin Kylie were the only other two kids in my grade. Laurie and I didn't like each other much when we were younger.

Laurie was actually the one who broke my foot in sixth grade. She won't admit that she broke it, but she did.

As I mentioned, Laurie and I were none too fond of each other when we were young. I thought she was stuck up, and she thought…well, I guess I'm not really sure what her problem was.

Anyway, since we lived out on a farm near each other, and we went to the same church, and we were the same ages, our parents thought we should be friends.

We had sleepovers, which we were forced to endure, as well as other gatherings. The first time I was forced to suffer through a sleep over with Laurie, I made her sleep on the floor on a mattress.

You see I have bunk beds.

I have perfectly good bunk beds.

I have an upper bed and a lower bed. Either of which would have been quite satisfactory, for a friend sleeping over, to sleep in.

I, however, did not want Laurie to have the comfort of my bunk beds.

I wanted her to sleep on a mattress on the floor.

We had a mattress standing on end, tucked behind our couch in the basement. My bedroom is in the basement, along with my brother's bedroom.

My sister, Lee, and I used to share a room, but she announced that I was too messy and moved her self out several years ago.

I think my sister has issues.

Viva le Resistance!

I was standing on the couch, reaching and pulling up on the mattress, trying to free it from behind the couch. Laurie decided to "help me." Laurie's idea of "helping me" was to pull the sheet on the mattress up and over my head, knocking me to the side.

I stepped blindly off the couch and my foot landed sideways on a sleeping bag, which was rolled up next to the couch.

SNAP!

My foot actually snapped in half!

To this day, she swears it was not her fault. Guess it could have been karma for making her sleep on the floor!

Viva le Resistance!

Laurie and I pretty much hated each other until track season last year. Our parents, being the thrifty beings that they were, demanded that we carpool. Our farms are over ten miles outside of town.

Not only did they force us to RIDE together, but we were also forced to WALK together, first! We had to walk TOGETHER from the high school, where the track was, to the mall.

It was over a mile!

Geez!

Despite this apparent torture, something good came out of the deal. Over diet coke and peanut M&M's every day, Laurie and I became the best of friends. Broken foot not forgotten, of course!

Laurie looks a lot, I mean a LOT, like Meg Ryan. She looks like a really young Meg Ryan. She has short ash blond hair and blue eyes. We spend most of our time together now. We are the two amigos, the best of friends; we are the daring duo of Center City!

Over there is Cara.

She is the girl with the dark brown long braids. Cara and I also rode the bus together when we were younger. Cara spent the night once and noticed that I had a small jar on my shelf.

Viva le Resistance!

The jar was full of fine ash and was clearly labeled Mt. St. Helen's. Mt. St. Helen was the volcano that erupted in the 1980's, spewing ASH. My grandmother had given me the jar when I was a little girl.

Cara looked at the jar and asked, "Who is Helen."

I said, "She was my dear, departed aunt. They called her a Saint because she was so sweet."

Cara looked at me and said, "Do you miss her?"

I wasn't sure how to respond. Let's just say that Cara is kind of naïve.

Viva le Resistance!

Cara is a year younger than we are, so we don't spend as much time together as we used to. The last time she spent the night my brother and his friend used a BB gun to protect themselves from her!

They didn't shoot her, or even point it at her for that matter. They just kept yelling, "Stay back, because we are armed!"

That is definitely not very nice, if you ask me.

I peeked into his room, to see what was going on, and saw Rick and David, my brother and his friend, crouched in a corner, hiding behind a BB gun. It was a little, tiny, innocent looking BB gun, like the one on that Christmas

Movie. The movie that the mom kept saying, "You'll put your eye out with that thing."

You see Rick and David are two years older than me.

Rick, my brother, has red hair and freckles. He lives and breathes to torture me. His favorite hobby is wetting my toothbrush so that I will think that he used it.

GROSS!

I finally figured out what he was doing. But until then, I went through a LOT of new toothbrushes!

David is Rick's best friend. They were friends way back when we lived in Hawkins, before we moved here. David spends the summers with us.

They are two peas in a pod.

They both prefer dorky flannel shirts, long sleeve flannel shirts; I mean they prefer them even in the summer! They both prefer to swim with their shoes on. They swim with their stinky, old tennis shoes with the holes in them, even in the swimming pool!

Viva le Resistance!

They both prefer irrigating boots as their favorite footwear. And they both hate to clean fish!

Rick has something called Asperger's Syndrome, so he doesn't always fit in either. Guess we have that in common.

Viva le Resistance!

Chapter Four

How funny is it that my older brother and his best friend get grossed out by a little fish blood?

I have never minded fish blood myself.

When I was four, I got my first fillet knife and BB gun. I always tell Rick that I am the son my father always wanted! I guess the torturing thing goes both ways in our family!

When we went camping last summer, Rick and David caught a huge mess of fish!

Viva le Resistance!

They brought it up to the camper as usual, and as usual, asked me to clean them.

Being the ever kind and loving sister that I am I said, "Sure. But only if you pay me."

A price was quickly negotiated. I began my work. Unfortunately, about three fish into the bunch, I slipped and stuck the end of my fillet knife through that skin flap thing, between by thumb and forefinger.

"OUCH, ouch, ouch, ouch," I cried.

It hurt even worse than the year before, when I had stepped on a treble hook and it had embedded itself in my foot!

Viva le Resistance!

I did, however, have to finish if I wanted to get paid.   So, while holding the bleeding part of my hand away from the fish, I continued to clean them.

It was not easy, I'm telling you.

Fish are very slippery and I was trying not to get my own blood in with the fillets!

About that time, my father walked up.

He took one look at me, and then he took one look at my hand.

He put his hand over his eyes and put his head down.

He rubbed his eyes for a few seconds.

Viva le Resistance!

He used his longest finger and thumb to kind of squish his eyes toward each other and apart.

Together, apart, together, apart....

Dad looked up and said, "Where are the boys?"

I said, "I think they are fishing off the dock."

"Go in, bandage that up, and put ice on it from the cooler," he replied.

Then, my dad turned and walked across the campground towards the water. I am not really sure what was said. But I know that the fish got cleaned, I got my money, and Rick and David never asked me to clean their fish again.

The night the two big babies huddled behind their little BB gun, Cara was on a roll.

David is not the best looking kid around. He is not the most athletic or even smartest.

But he was, after all, there.

Which, in Cara's book, was as good as it gets!

Cara started by calling his name.

"DA-vid," she'd say.

"DAAAAA-vid."

No answer came from the bedroom, where David was with Rick. There was a very hushed silence all of the sudden.

Viva le Resistance!

"DAAAAA-vid, I Looooooove you," Cara crooned.

"DA-vid, I honestly love you," she said in a sing-song voice.

The hushed silence continued.

"Daaaaaaa-vid. I know you are in there."

Nothing.

"Daaaaa-vid. I want to see you."

Nothing.

"Okay David. I'm coming for a kiss," she announced with a heave to her feet.

Scrambling, door slamming, shuffling, things being knocked over.

What was going on in there?

Viva le Resistance!

"David. I said I'm COMING for you,"
Cara continued in her sing-songy voice.

And then, the yelling began.

"Stay back!"

"We are armed!"

"Don't come in here!"

"I mean it!"

"Don't even think about it!"

On and on it went.

Back and forth, they took turns yelling.
Rick and David carried on forever, it seemed.

Oddly enough, as soon as they started in,
Cara rolled over and went to sleep with a little
smirk on her face.

What a hoot.

Viva le Resistance!

She was just messing with the goofballs.

Later in the night, several hours later in fact, David snuck out of the room. He kept his back to the door and faced us, as he quietly sidestepped his way out of the room. When he made it to the hallway, I heard him tumble and stumble up the stairs.

You see, the only bathroom was upstairs.

The poor guy had to hold it, until he thought it was safe to leave the room!

Chapter Five

Ah.

Here we are.

Music class.

Music class is one of the highlights of the day. It's really kind of sad, because our teacher is pretty much fair game for us and our pranks. His name is Mr. Harlin.

Mr. Harlin is about 5'4" or 5'5" and maybe weighs 110lbs-soaking wet. Mr. Harlin is probably in his early 50's, but he seriously looks like he may have passed away decades ago, and is being controlled and animated by animatronics.

Mr. Harlin has stringy, dingy, graying hair that never looks washed. It hangs woefully in his eyes. Mr. Harlin keeps a metal comb, wrapped in a tissue, in his front shirt pocket.

When he gets flustered, Mr. Harlin reaches into his pocket, while repeatedly clearing his throat.

He takes the comb and carefully removes the tissue.

Mr. Harlin nervously runs the metal comb repeatedly through the front of his hair, somehow leaving it looking more disheveled than when he started.

He then carefully refolds the tissue around the comb and slips it back into his front pocket.

Mr. Harlin, like many men his age, feels the need to pull his brown, polyester pants roughly up to his armpits. He further demonstrates the need to frequently tug at his belt, shifting his pants from side to side, which dislodges the brown, plaid buttoned to his chin shirt.

Finally, the process starts over, as he goes through the ritual of re-tucking, readjusting, and resettling himself.

Viva le Resistance!

Furthermore, Mr. Harlin has a very distracting habit with his lips. He constantly, almost like a tic, runs his tongue across his palate, behind his front teeth, up across the front of his top teeth (with his lips still closed), with the grand finale being the protrusion of his tongue out, down, and back in.

Wash, rinse, and repeat.

Over and over and over, he does it.

It's sad really.

I guess that's why he is the student body's number one target for pranks, needling, and general merriment.

The class is your typical music class. It doubles as a band room and has a large storage closet, for instruments, on the far wall. The back of the room is lined with windows. The seats are arranged in a semi-circle, with Mr. Harlin and his piano at the front.

I've never been able to figure out exactly why Mr. Harlin sits with the piano between him and his students.

Protection?

Avoidance?

Clueless?

The piano is one of those old uprights that inhibit his view of the class. He repeatedly sticks his head around the right side, to redirect or otherwise engage us. For the most part, he sits happily behind his piano pounding away, oblivious to the daily shenanigans going on around him.

Last week it began with the usual. Mr. Harlin started with the pulling, shifting, tucking, lip smacking routine, along with the usual attendance taking, and admonitions to take our seats and be quiet.

When he was seated firmly behind the piano and the music began, Sam leaned his chair back precariously. He carefully and quietly reached around behind himself to open the window farthest to the right back corner of the room. This was, of course, the window farthest from Mr. Harlin and best concealed by the upright piano back.

Slowly, slowly, up went the window.

Oops.

Stop. He's peering around.

Whew!

Viva le Resistance!

Again, slowly, slowly, up went the window.

Quickly and quietly, Lane snaked out the open window, dropped to the ground, and tore around the side of the school. Sam surreptitiously slid the window back into place. All the while Mr. Harlin played obliviously along and the class continued to sing as if nothing were out of the ordinary.

A few minutes tick by.

The class continues to sing.

Mr. Harlin is now really getting into the song. He rocks back and forth, while simultaneously pounding out the tune and smacking his lips.

Viva le Resistance!

Back and forth, eyes half closed, not a clue in the world, he continues on.

Then, a knock at the door interrupts the rousing rendition. Up Mr. Harlin goes, while glancing back at us with the, "You had better behave yourselves or you'll be sorry" look that most teachers give when an unexpected guest arrives.

Mr. Harlin reaches for the doorknob as he glances around at us for the final squinty warning, and whom does he find?

Standing in the hallway, is Lane, looking as innocent as can be.

Viva le Resistance!

First, surprise flits across Mr. Harlin's face, followed almost immediately by confusion, concern, and finally annoyance.

Had he let Lane go to the bathroom or his locker?

Was Lane even here when we called attendance?

Hmmmm…you could almost see the thoughts crossing through his mind. A brief shrug followed and then Mr. Harlin said,

"Back to your seat young man."

A little throat clearing, a little lip smacking, a brief pants and belt adjustment, and he was headed back towards the piano. Back down Mr. Harlin sat. A stretch of the arm, another round of lip smacking, and we were back off and running.

Mr. Harlin played with abandonment, the class belted out the tune with gusto, and Sam reached carefully behind himself.

Up, up, up went the window.

Silent, silent, silently it moved.

Quickly, and with stealth, out the window Lane flew again.

Mr. Harlin peered momentarily around the side of the piano, while continuing the song. Innocence radiated out of the class, as we appeared to be giving our musical best.

Sam, again, carefully slid the window back into place. Again, all the while Mr.

Harlin played along, without a clue and the class continued to sing as if nothing were amuck.

Again the minutes ticked by.

Viva le Resistance!

The class continued to sing.

Mr. Harlin, again getting caught up in the song, rocks back and forth while simultaneously pounding out the tune and smacking his lips. Back and forth, eyes half closed, not a clue in the world he continues on.

Another knock at the door interrupts the performance. This time there is some squirming and giggling from the class. Up Mr. Harlin goes while again glancing back at us with the, "You had better behave yourselves or you'll be sorry," look that he threw at us before.

Viva le Resistance!

Mr. Harlin reaches for the doorknob and glances around at us for the final squinty warning, and who does he find...again?

There he is!

Again!

Lane is standing there looking totally innocent. Again the surprise flits across Mr. Harlin's face followed by the same confusion, concern, and annoyance.

"All right class. What is going on here?" Mr. Harlin demands.

Most of us look down at our shoes or become intensely interested in the music sheets. Sam, who always cracks, begins to

65

laugh while trying to muffle the sound with his hand.

His face, of course, turns beet red.

Sam can never hide anything.

Mr. Harlin glares.

"Lane, what were you doing in the hall?" he asks, while placing his left hand on Lane's right shoulder and squeezing.

Lane, who also cannot pull anything off without the telltale giggles and his face reddening, replies, "What do you mean?"

He ducks down, snorts through his nose, glances up through is lashes at Sam, and turns away, stifling an all out guffaw with his hand.

Viva le Resistance!

"You know EXACTLY what I mean young man. Do you need to have a visit with Principal Johns?" Mr. Harlin intones, while nervously shifting, tugging, and pulling at his pants with his free right hand.

Lane managed to pull it together and look innocently up at Mr. Harlin.

"You said I could go to my locker," he barely gets out, while struggling to keep a straight face.

Sam is now rolling back and forth, holding his sides, beet red in the face, and giggling uncontrollably, albeit quietly.

Mr. Harlin glances sharply up at Sam, followed by a brief glaring perusal of the class.

Most of us were still staring at our shoes and trying not to break into fits of laughter.

"Back to your seat young man."

Mr. Harlin pauses, reaches into his front shirt pocket, and withdraws the silver metal comb. He unwraps it and swipes it viciously through the front of his hair, while trying to stair everyone down at once.

Mr. Harlin carefully folds the tissue back around the comb, never allowing his gaze to stray from us. He slides the tissue covered comb into his front shirt pocket, all the while, subconsciously running his tongue across his palate, behind his front teeth, up across the front of his top teeth (with his lips still closed), and finally protruding his tongue out, down, and back in.

Smack, smack, smack.

Finally, he heads back to the piano, and with another stretch of the arm, another round of lip smacking, and away we go!

What do you think happened next?

Did they have the guts to try it again?

Would Mr. Harlin be so dense as to allow himself to look like a buffoon again?

Oh yeah, they did.

And he did.

I wonder what they will pull today!

Chapter Six

"All right class, settle down," Mr. Harlin is getting ready for roll.

"Sam?"

"Here," Sam calls back.

"Annie?"

"Here," I call, glad that I am sitting next to Sam.

"Lane?" Mr. Harlin continues to call the rest of the names on the list.

Viva le Resistance!

The only one missing is Katie, and I am hoping she has head lice again.

Not very nice of me, I know. It's just that Katie has a way of hurting people, while looking innocent and lovely.

No one would ever suspect her of duplicity.

Like when she demolished Tori for no real reason. Tori is, as I mentioned earlier, a little on the heavy side. She is nice and smart. She hangs with the cliquey's, but still treats other kids nicely.

Tori and I used to be pretty good friends, in her pre-cliquey years. Tori was sitting in her desk, when Katie walked by and kind of ran into her. Katie wasn't watching where she was going and stumbled into the desk in front of her, knocking some papers to the floor.

Some of the class laughed, and Lane asked, "Walk much Katie? Or do you just read about it in the funny papers?"

Katie did not find it amusing, but she still pasted on the blinding smile. She gave a little giggle and leaned down to Tori, like she was just straightening up the papers she had knocked off the desk.

"You did that on purpose, you fat cow," she sneered.

Tori gasped. She had not done anything on purpose and she was stunned.

Viva le Resistance!

"You know," Katie continued slyly, "You may be older than me, but you'll also always be fatter than me."

Tori's eyes filled with tears. Katie and Tori were, after all, both in the cliquey's and supposedly friends.

The comment was so odd and out of place, but Katie had already flounced off, before Tori could even respond.

Viva le Resistance!

"Settle down and turn to page six," Mr. Harlin calls out, as he clears his throat loudly, and spends several seconds with the strange lip smacking routine. He runs his tongue across his palate, behind his front teeth, up across the front of his top teeth (with his lips still closed), with the grand finale, again, being the protrusion of his tongue out, down, and back in.

I ask you, what is with that?

Mr. Harlin seats himself behind the piano and begins playing.

The class begins to sing in unison.

Oh no.

They are at it again.

Viva le Resistance!

As Mr. Harlin gets into his music, Ted, who is sitting next to the band storage closet door, quickly opens the door.

Tom shoots in.

Ted closes the door and keeps singing.

Again, Ted whips open the door.

Lane darts in.

Close.

Ted opens.

Ron is next.

And so on and so on, until it is just Sam, Laurie, Ted, a few others, and me left singing.

Coming to the end of the song, Mr. Harlin nods with a satisfied smile and stands up.

Viva le Resistance!

He looks up and his jaw falls open.

When he started playing he had a classroom full of students. Now, he has just a handful of us left!

His face turned red.

He sputtered.

He looked at Sam, who was also turning red, and giggling uncontrollably. He looked at Ted, who was trying so hard not to laugh; he fell out of his chair.

I honestly don't see why the poor man bothers coming to work!

"Where," he stutters.

"Ahem," he clears his throat.

"Where are they THIS time?!" he roars.

The poor man is actually shaking.

Sam can't help himself and he glances towards the closet door.

Mr. Harlin gives a quick tug to his pants and a twisting adjustment to his belt. He then sets his chinless jaw, and marches determinedly towards the band room closet door.

The rest of us are dead silent in anticipation.

Mr. Harlin yanks open the door.

Bad move.

In addition to the bodies now stashed in the band room closet, there are also multiple band instruments to include drums, tubas,

French horns, and so on. The band room closet was not designed to hold all of the instruments, as well as all of the bodies now crammed in and on top of them.

For one hushed instant, nothing happened.

Mr. Harlin stared, we watched, and nothing.

But, this was only for an instant.

Then, in a mountainous tumble of bodies and band instruments, the avalanche began. Out they fell, rolled, and bounced, squirmed, squealed, cracked, and splayed.

Viva le Resistance!

Poor Mr. Harlin took the brunt of it and was buried under the pile of students and instruments.

I'm thinking today may be the final straw for Mr. Harlin.

As he squirmed his way out from under the throng, while smacking, pulling at his clothes, anxiously smoothing the front of his hair down, and simultaneously reaching for his comb with the other hand, he barks, "This afternoon, after school, you will all be spending time with me. And you will be spending time with Mr. Johns who I will be inviting to join us!"

Viva le Resistance!

He added the last statement as an afterthought, I think.

I believe he is going to "invite" Mr. Johns, the principal, as a protector from us!

The bell rings.

Everyone, grumbling, trudges out into the hallway and on to the next class.

Guess I'd better call my mom and tell her I'm going to need a ride home tonight.

Chapter Seven

Teachers aren't the only ones to face harassment at the hands of pranksters. This morning, Kylie was sitting on the bus, minding her own business, when Jimmy popped around the seat and sat down next to her.

"What do you want?" she asked with a wary look on her face.

Jimmy is not the type of kid who sits down next to you because he wants to be friends or share casual conversation. Jimmy is the type of kid who sits down next to you, to put gum in your hair, or an "I'm *stoopid*" sign on your back!

She asked again, "Really Jimmy, what do you want?"

Jimmy looked directly into her eyes, while pointing at the floor of the bus.

To Kylie's horror, she saw her purse on the floor and a female product had fallen out!

How utterly embarrassing it was for her.

Poor Kylie turned every shade of red, while Jimmy laughed and pointed at it, lying there on the floor.

Louder and louder he laughed, bouncing up and down in his seat, drawing the attention of everyone on the bus, to include the bus driver, who was glaring balefully at Jimmy and Kylie.

She shrank down and frantically tried to scoop everything up and into her purse, so no one else could see.

But, Jimmy just wouldn't let it go.

"What's the matter Kylie?" he started in.

"What do you need that for Kylie?" he continued.

"Hey Kylie is that," he was cut short.

You see, at that point Sam had moved closer to their seat. Steadily, he had moved up behind Jimmy, never once laughing at Kylie's embarrassment and humiliation.

"What's the problem here?" he intoned in that wonderful voice of his.

Grabbing onto the back of Jimmy's neck, in a bit of a vice-like manner, he whispered, "We don't hurt girls' feelings on this bus, Jerk."

In a louder voice, Sam said, "No. She doesn't need it. She brought it for you!"

The whole bus erupted in laughter.

Even the normally cranky bus driver seemed to crack a little smile.

Jimmy slunk down in his seat and we didn't hear another word out of him!

You can see why I find Sam so yummy!

Viva le Resistance!

He has always been a bit of a goof. He isn't really the cutest boy. But, he never fails to come to the rescue of someone being picked on.

We have English next. Mrs. Mark is okay.

She is Paula's mom.

Paula, if you remember, was my odiferous friend from 6th grade.

Not many people mess around in Mrs. Mark's class.

She is big.

She is big and loud, and more than a little scary.

Viva le Resistance!

Mrs. Mark can command silence and control, with a mere glance.

Mrs. Mark's favorite of all activities, is sentence diagramming.

Why, you might ask?

I have no idea.

Tonight is the first dance of the year. It is very hard to concentrate on diagramming sentences, when all I can think about is whether or not Sam will ask me to dance!

"Hey," I hear a whisper from behind me.

"Hey, Annie,"

I glance up to see if Mrs. Mark is looking. I do not want to experience her wrath for talking in class!

Viva le Resistance!

"Annie," whispered a little louder this time.

I turn around and find myself staring into those beautiful blue eyes! Sam!

Oh no. I hope he can't tell that I was daydreaming about him!

"Hey Annie, are you going to the dance tonight?" he asks in a quiet voice.

Oh joy!

Oh wonderful wonderful day!

I think the birds are even singing a little louder!

Nonchalantly I reply, "I think so, why?"

"No reason," he says, glancing down shyly, "I was just wondering."

Viva le Resistance!

Oh happy day!

"How about you?" I ask in an I-could-care-less tone of voice.

"Yeah," he whispers, "Katie and Ron asked me to go with them and Julie."

What!?

Are you kidding me?!

Julie?

My mind is racing!

Julie is another of the cliquey's. She and Katie are identical in personality and sheer meanness.

Julie is tall and slim.

She has green eyes and dark wavy hair.

Viva le Resistance!

She can burp the alphabet, but other than
that has no real redeeming traits. She likes to
gossip and steal other girls' boyfriends.

These are her hobbies.

How can my Sam be going with Julie?

"I'm not sure I want to go with them
though," he says as if waiting for my response.

Deep breaths, deep breaths.

Don't overreact.

"Really?" I throw out there, as if my
heart weren't in my throat and my palms
sweaty.

He can't, he can't, he can't, he can't.....

"Nah," he looks up at me through his
eyelashes, "I'm not really into Julie."

Viva le Resistance!

The sun is brighter, the sky more blue....

"Annie...," he starts.

"Annie, Sam, you both need to get back to your papers. I do not want to hear another peep out of either of you," Mrs. Mark bellows.

NOOOOOOO.

What was he going to say?

What was he going to ask?

Does he like me?

Ugh!

The agony!

Why is it that teachers seem to have such great timing under circumstances like this?

After class, I can wait until after class.

Viva le Resistance!

Surely he will pick up where he left off.
Won't he?

Chapter Eight

The bell rings.

We all stand, grab our books, and shove and push our way out to the hallway.

Mrs. Mark glares over us, like the bald eagle on the Muppets!

A few weeks ago Mrs. Mark caught Laurie and I talking in class.

Not that this is an unusual phenomenon, since Laurie and I frequently get caught talking in class.

After all, we have a lot to say!

Viva le Resistance!

We believe that communication should be actively encouraged. It is Laurie's and my belief, that there is not enough healthy communication in this world!

That is why my dad had to install a second phone line at our house.

He said he just got tired of asking me to, "Please just GET OFF the phone for one lousy minute!"

I think he was being a bit melodramatic, but if it gets me my own phone, who am I to judge?

Anyway, Mrs. Mark snuck up on us, as we were having a healthy discussion about the merits of straightening iron versus chemically straightening our hair.

I thought that the modicum of permanency, that chemical straightening allowed, and, therefore, time saved, outweighed the damage and dryness it did to a person's hair.

Laurie, however, was just launching into her opinion regarding the options for multiple styles if a straightening iron were used, instead of chemicals, since it wasn't as permanent, when the large shadow loomed over us.

Uh oh.

We both glanced guiltily at each other and then up at Mrs. Mark.

Viva le Resistance!

Do you know that she grabbed each of us by the hair and then bonked our heads together?

Can you believe that?

I thought there were laws against that sort of thing!

My mom thought it was funny and said we spend enough time on the phone that we shouldn't need to talk in class.

Okay.

Out in the hallway.

Where is Sam?

Oh no! He is all the way down the hall, surrounded by his gaggle of bagmen!

Viva le Resistance!

Now I may never know what he was about to ask me!

Ach!

The agony of it all!

(A moment of silent reflection and agonized expression.)

Oh well.

On to Science, I guess.

Mr. Parry is great. He looks like a leprechaun. He is little, sort of round in the middle, has red hair, and kind of pointy ears. All he is missing is the funny shoes and green outfit with matching hat!

Viva le Resistance!

We've been getting ready to dissect frogs. Mr. Parry lectured us on anatomy and safety all last week.

He explained the procedures and cautioned about not screwing around, while looking at each of the bagmen.

Sam and Lane giggled.

I really don't mind dissecting a frog. I used to go frog hunting, with my dad, all of the time.

Stuff like that doesn't bother me much.

However, Mr. Parry has teamed us up, since apparently the school is too cheap to buy each of us our own frog!

Viva le Resistance!

Each group consists of a boy and a girl.
Maybe this teaming thing is really a ruse, so
girls don't have to get grossed out?

Sneaky Mr. Parry, very sneaky, I get
what you are doing here.

I am partnered with Keith, the mild-
mannered kind-of-looks-like-me Keith. He is
the newest member of the bagmen, and pretty
smart guy, Keith.

Cool.

I like Keith.

Viva le Resistance!

Mr. Parry walks around each of the tables, and hands us what looks kind of like a 9x13 cake pan, with blackish hard wax stuff in the bottom.

Mr. Parry then walks around each of the tables and provides us with a scalpel, some stick pins, and this thing with a wooden handle and a nail looking thing in the end.

Mr. Parry said that since our frogs are already dead and in formalin, we wouldn't actually have to use the nail looking thing, to pith our frogs.

Which, I guess, is good for us, because as I look around the room, I am already seeing some queasy looking faces.

If we did, Mr. Parry explained, we would use the instrument to pierce the brain and sever the spinal cord, to instantly kill the frogs, without pain.

Cool.

No pain is a good thing, I guess, if you are a frog about to be chopped up by a bunch of middle school students.

I look around, trying to see how Laurie is taking all of this.

Viva le Resistance!

My view is blocked.

Bummer.

I turn towards Tori.

Tori is watching Mr. Parry, with an expectant look on her face.

Tori is kind of like me, when it comes to hunting and fishing stuff. We both have older brothers, and dads who like to take us camping, fishing, hunting, and all that other stuff that most girls hate.

Tori and I actually went through hunter safety courses together, a couple of years ago. We were, of course, the only girls.

There were about twenty boys and four instructors in the class. I out-shot everyone in

the class and three of the instructors. I tied
with the fourth.

It was great.

We used to have so much fun together.

Then Tori joined the cliquey's.

It's been downhill from there.

Next, Mr. Parry walked behind the lab
sink in the center middle of the front of the
room, and lifted up a big white bucket with the
skull and cross bones sign, used on poisonous
stuff.

Here we go!

Mr. Parry stops in front of each
workstation and pulls out a drippy, smelly, stiff
looking frog. He lifts it by one foot and places

it in each of our cake pans, with the hard black wax thing in the bottom.

His legs are stretched out and stiff. One leg is hanging over the side of our cake pan and sort of dripping onto the papers underneath.

I stare at my poor frog's corpse and think he probably should have a name. His death clearly wasn't very dignified, and it does seem like the least I could do.

I briefly turn to look up at Keith, to get his input.

Uh oh.

Keith doesn't look so good.

Keith REALLY doesn't look so good.

Viva le Resistance!

"MR. PARRY," I yell.

"MR. PAR-RY we have a small problem here," I say as I'm grabbing onto Keith's shirt.

I now understand what they mean when the say "he went down like a sack of potatoes."

I'd heard the saying, but I had never really given it much thought.

Keith's face is turning roughly the color of the pea soup stuff that my grandma insists on making on Christmas Eve, that no one will ever eat.

He is now becoming kind of gray.

He is turning gray like a black and white picture and his eyes sort of seem to be sinking back in his head.

Viva le Resistance!

This is definitely not good.

Next his gaze seemed to leave my face and peer somewhere over my right shoulder.

His body began to sway a little.

He swayed back and then upright.

He swayed to the side and then upright.

Whoa.

He swayed to the other side and then upright.

Suddenly, he looked me directly in the eyes, and then his eyes flew open and he just went down.

I was trying to hold on to him, but seriously, just like a sack of potatoes he was down.

Viva le Resistance!

Unfortunately, on the way down, he managed to clip the solid black top of our workstation with his chin.

Chaos ensues.

The screeching of chairs, the knocking over of workstations and books, as everyone tries quickly to get to Keith, who now looks very peaceful.

His face is pale now, instead of gray, and he simply looks like he's sleeping.

Well, peaceful except for that pool of blood forming under his head from the gash on his chin.

Uh oh.

Viva le Resistance!

Looking around the room I'm seeing a lot of people with that same grayish shade.

I wonder if every year, dissecting frogs is such a drama!

Finally, I can see Laurie.

Her eyes are open so wide, that it looks like her eyebrows have disappeared somewhere into her hairline.

Mr. Parry is scrambling to take care of Keith, calm everyone down, and send someone to the office for the nurse.

She arrives in a flurry of gauze and motherly concern.

Viva le Resistance!

Quickly and efficiently she rouses Keith, bandages his chin, and walks him out to call his mother.

I bet Keith has a note tomorrow excusing him from dissecting, just like some kids bring to get them out of P.E.

Chapter Nine

The rest of the morning has gone rather uneventfully. We are headed through the lunch line.

I've found out that Laurie's middle name means "wild-cow" in Hebrew, or some other language.

From now on, I think I shall call her, "Beulah."

Hey, "Beulah," I test it out.

She is pretending not to hear me.

"Beulah," I say more emphatically.

She turns without comment, but isn't smiling.

Odd.

"Hey, Beu," I am cut short by a quick jab to the solar plexus by my best friend, who shall now also be known as "wild-cow."

Maybe it's too soon.

She may need more time to adjust.

We shuffle along like meat on a conveyor belt.

Step to the side, get your tray. Step to the side, take your milk. Step to the side, napkins and silverware. Step to the side...and so it goes.

Viva le Resistance!

I squeeze into the seat between Beu..I mean Laurie and Tori. We are all kind of mashed together on these benches attached to the tables. There aren't individual chairs and they don't pull out.

So you have to lift your tray over the heads of people already sitting, trying to balance and not drop any food on the unwitting friends below, while hoisting a leg up in the air and trying to insinuate it up and over the bench, next to whoever is sitting there.

Then, while kind of straddling the bench, settle your tray, pick up your other foot and try to tuck it in and under the table as well.

Viva le Resistance!

All of this, while everyone else is also completing the same gyrations. It's amazing that anyone ends up with food still on his or her tray!

As I am getting seated, I just happen to glance up.

Blue eyes.

Blue eyes staring back at me from three tables over.

I can't breathe!

Sam!

More shifting and seating, with people walking by and I lose eye contact.

Darn it.

Viva le Resistance!

Now I can't see him at all, since the rest of the bagmen have closed ranks around him and Lane.

The cliquey's, minus Tori who is sitting by me, also seat themselves impeding my view.

"Nooooooo....," my brain is screaming.

Oh well.

We begin discussing the Science incident, when Tori reaches behind her.

She turns back to me.

"Here," she says, while thrusting something towards me.

Tori doesn't even look up.

With her left hand, she lifts her fork to her mouth; head down, with dark bangs falling over her eyes, and with her right hand shoving something at me.

"Thanks," I say reaching out.

It is a folded note.

Odd.

Notes are, as you are probably aware, forbidden. Why, I can't really tell you. I believe that encouraging note writing would increase our written language skills.

Wouldn't this, in fact, be a GOOD thing?

I look around to see who might have passed the note along, but didn't see anyone watching. I looked towards the lunch ladies to make sure that they wouldn't try to snatch it up before I could read it.

The lunch ladies seemed engrossed in conversation with the maintenance guy.

I slowly open the note.

"Do you like me?" That's all it said. "Do you like me?"

Again, I looked around, and didn't see anyone watching.

That's weird.

I turned the note over to read the front. Maybe they'd passed it to the wrong person. Maybe I was supposed to pass it on and not read it.

Viva le Resistance!

No.

The front says 'Annie.'

"Do you like me?" I read it again.

Confused, I wrinkle my brow and look around.

Oh my goodness.

I can't breathe.

Could it be?

Could it?

Oh please, oh please, oh please…..

I slowly look up. Bagmen and cliquey's hinder my view.

Is it from him?

Is it?

Could it be?

"Oh please, oh please, oh please," my heart continues chanting.

As the bagmen part, and the cliquey's lean in to hear their conversation, my view becomes unobstructed.

Sam.

It's as if the heavens have parted behind him.

There is a light, illuminating his beautiful face, and tipping his shiny, strawberry-blond hair, gold.

It's as if the entire cafeteria has gone silent and cherubs are humming a beautiful tune.

Okay maybe not, but this is my moment!

Viva le Resistance!

He's looking at me.

Suddenly all fades away and it's as if a camera with a zoom lens brings his adorable face closer to mine.

He's looking at me with his eyebrows up.

He wrote it?

Is it possible?

Sam nods and looks expectantly.

He wrote it!

He wrote it. He wrote it. He wrote it!

Oh my.

I feel my face turning red.

Sam looks down.

He looks sad.

Viva le Resistance!

Oh no! Look up!

Look up. Look up. Look up!

Sam looks up, and our eyes meet.

I nod slowly. His face brightens.

The bell.

The bell is ringing, and I have not eaten,
but who cares? It's the greatest day ever!

Wait.

Wait just a minute.

"Do you like me?"

Just, "Do you like me?"

Oh no! He never said that he likes me!

What have I done? Never ever, ever
admit that you like a boy before he admits that
he likes you!

119

Viva le Resistance!

That is one of, if not the most crucial, of all emotional cardinal rules!

Chapter Ten

The world comes crashing into harsh focus.

The jostling of hundreds of bodies, trying to get out of the cafeteria at the same time, along with the enormity of what I'd just done, smashing into me.

Laurie accidentally bumps into my arm and I barely look up.

"What's wrong?" she asks.

No reply.

I can't reply.

What have I done?

"Annie, what is with you?" She intones again.

"Are you alright?" she takes my arm.

I nod miserably and take my arm out of her grasp.

"Yeah I'm okay," I mumble as we pick up our trays and head towards the door of the cafeteria, milling along with everyone else.

"Are you going to tell me what's wrong?" she persists.

I nod numbly.

"As you know, I really like Sam," I begin.

"Sam?" Tori buts in with her mouth full so it really sounds like, "Smaum?"

Viva le Resistance!

"Yeah Sam," I reply as Cara bumps into me from behind, almost spilling my tray onto Laurie.

"Sorry," she grins.

Tori is kind of mumbling because she is trying desperately to eat the last of her fries on her tray, before she has to put her tray on the counter for the cooks to clean up.

Swallowing hard, she says without looking up, "Oh, I heard he's going with Julie."

What?!

I almost drop my tray.

"Hey!" Jimmy exclaims from behind me.

Viva le Resistance!

"Move it will ya?" he whines, "I don't want to be late again."

My stomach is really rolling now.

He's going with Julie the alphabet-burping-snide friend of Katie?

He told me that he WASN'T interested in Julie, in Mrs. Mark's classroom.

Oh no, is this pay back for my abduction of the precious Phat Times 20 book bags? Could he really be that cruel?

Jimmy whines again, "Hey, I'm trying to get through here."

I mutter something incoherent with some semblance of, "Sorry."

Viva le Resistance!

I move numbly and robotically through the line, as I am bumped, jostled, elbowed, and generally shoved through the line towards the cook's clean up window.

I am oblivious to the commotion.

How could he?

To the right are two overflowing gray garbage cans lined with clear bags for dumping milk cartons, napkins, left over foods, or any other miscellaneous trash.

If you look even remotely closely, you'll see the telltale stains of countless "missed targets" and the smudge of dried milk, food, and various other disgusting drippage trails, snaking down the sides.

Viva le Resistance!

Next on the left, although now obscured
by the throng of overly eager middle schoolers
dashing for the exit, are the trays for dirty
silverware.

Above the trays, hangs a sort of sci-fi,
scary-looking long hose, with, what appears to
be, a large showerhead attached.

Periodically, one of the hair-net
enshrouded lunch ladies would hoist the giant
hose-thing and, disinterestedly, spray the food
encrusted silverware, getting some, but not all,
of the gross particles off of the silverware.

Unfortunately for anyone standing in
front of the trays, most if not all of the gooey

mishmash of disgusting stuff would fly out, slathering the unsuspecting innocent bystander.

One must be quick and wary when passing the apathetic hose spraying lunch lady, or one will end up wearing some nasty stuff for the rest of the day.

One dim and dreary day, the cliquey's, en-herd, forgot to be vigilant and quick on their feet, when traversing this treacherous trail.

As you can imagine, the tragedy of the beautiful ones being besmirched by anything as heinous as the spray of old food is almost too much to bear!

I can't begin to describe the carnage and hysteria on that bleak and infamous day.

Viva le Resistance!

It was awesome!

Clearly, still in a state of shock over the recent development of my beloved, I am in a vulnerable state.

Luckily, Laurie, my ever-protective friend, spots the potential for a major fashion faux pas on my part, (i.e., au de food slop ala lunch lady).

Tori, who is still swiping up the last of her ketchup and loudly sucking the remnants from her fingers, deftly slides by the silverware tray without incident.

Cara, who managed to scoot by me when she bumped into me earlier, also managed to escape the ever-impending spray.

Viva le Resistance!

She gives us a quick wave over her shoulder, after sliding her tray to rest on top of the others waiting to be cleaned.

Laurie is moving closer to her turn, but is keeping an eye on me, as I am clearly still staring blindly, after hearing Tori's news about Sam and Julie.

Sam.

How could you?

Again Laurie tries, "Annie really, what is up with you girl?"

Laurie turns away from me briefly; to toss her silverware into the tray and set her used lunch tray on top of Cara's in the pile.

Quickly she turns back, just in time to see catastrophe looming!

I take a step forward, after placing my unopened milk, unused napkin, and uneaten food into the giant gray trash bin. I come close to bumping into the slimy side of the container, when Jimmy again tries to snake his way around me.

"Watch it loser," he sneers.

"Jerk," I automatically reply without thought as this sort of conversation frequently occurs when Jimmy is around.

Almost as if in slow motion, I turn back towards the silverware tray. A hairnet lady is clearly visible, but in my misery, I do not notice.

My vision is slightly blurred.

My left foot moves forward, while my head is still turned slightly to the right, towards the trash bin, watching as my untouched food sinks into the muck.

Still, in a semi-suspended state (or so it seems), I start to look forward, as my right foot moves ever so slightly past my left foot, trudging closer to the tray, my hair gently swaying against my cheek as I turn....

Chapter Eleven

Bam!

Laurie has plastered me against the wall! My head hits the yellow-orange tiles that cover the wall, across from the spray happy lunch lady.

Owwww.

Laurie had spotted the lunch lady reaching for the hose and looked to me.

She saw me, still dazed, and clearly unaware of the impending deluge of water spray and inedible muck about to permeate my person.

Viva le Resistance!

Laurie, sensing my inability to defend myself from the onslaught, launches herself at me with no thought to her own safety or that of the semi-new shirt she was wearing.

Unmindful of the danger to herself, or more importantly that of her clothes, Laurie throws herself to my defense.

"Noooooooo!" She reaches out her left hand towards me, while simultaneously using her right hand to slightly wrap around the cool tiles of the wall next to the lunch lady, and PUSH off with surprising strength.

With her hand still outstretched, Laurie's left shoulder shifts forward and the lower half of her body follows. She is boomeranged across the small hallway towards me.

Laurie flings herself through the path of the advancing spray, head shaking back and forth with the continued cry, "Noooooooo!" Her body smashes into me heaving me backwards with unexpected power, and an inelegant, "Ooomph" from me.

The sound came deep from my diaphragm when she collided with my midsection and my head smacked into the wall.

Did I mention that Laurie is great?

As we flew backwards into the glossed surface of the tile, my arms reflexively reached out for something to hold onto.

Viva le Resistance!

Unfortunately what my outstretched left hand found to hold onto was none other than the side of Jimmy's head.

Too bad Kylie isn't here to see this!

After the bus incident this morning, she would have really enjoyed the spectacle coming!

Jimmy had been unsuccessful in his attempts to skirt around me or push me out of the way earlier.

Consequently, he had been in the process of dumping his tray into the gray trash bin nearest me. The trash bin had one of those huge clear liners to hold the food.

Viva le Resistance!

The liner had been put in slightly askew and it had a sort of puckered pocket formed that hung outside of the bin itself. In this trashcan liner pouch-like area, had gathered a curious mess of milk, soaked bread, smashed fries, and what looked like it had once been mixed fruit, but now resembled baby barf.

Upon impact and my involuntary reaching for balance, followed by the connection between my hand and Jimmy's head, a series of unfortunate events occurred.

Well, I say unfortunate in that had it happened to anyone BUT Jimmy, it would have been unfortunate.

Since it was Jimmy…..

Viva le Resistance!

Because everything transpired so
quickly, I did not have the proper time to relish
the situation. I'm sure in the future I will look
back on this as one of my fonder memories!

Laurie tackled me into the wall.

"Oomph!"

My hand shot out for balance.

My hand caught the side of Jimmy's
head.

Jimmy's head had been bent forward
concentrating on avoiding the disgusting food
filled trash bag receptacle thing, hanging
precariously near his leg, while he emptied his
tray.

Viva le Resistance!

The force of my hand meeting the side of his head overbalanced Jimmy.

He toppled forward.

Jimmy's right hand, which had been holding the tray, disappeared into the filthy food and trash filled bin.

His left foot shot out from underneath him, due to a slick spot of ketchup on the floor.

And then the coups de grace, the piece de resistance, the crème de la crème, the greatest that ever could have happened to Jimmy, happened.

Jimmy's face fell forward landing with a splat in the middle of that disgusting pouch hanging from the side of the trash bin!

Viva le Resistance!

Splat!

"Mmmmph!" Jimmy struggled to regain his balance.

I can only imagine that he was trying to keep his mouth shut and not breathe in!

Viva le Resistance!

Jimmy couldn't immediately regain his balance, so his initial thrashing about smeared and smooshed the gooey stuff about.

The goop oozed out around his neckline.

Jimmy eventually got his feet underneath him, pried the muck and plastic away from his face, and slowly pushed himself up to a standing position.

Everyone was silent watching the scene unfold with eyes wide!

Even the lunch lady paused still holding the hose thing.

Chapter Twelve

Jimmy struggled to regain his footing.

His feet were slightly more than shoulder-width apart. His knees were bent slightly out and his head hung forward. His arms were at first up in the air like if a cop had just said to him, "Stick 'em up."

Then he lowered his arms somewhat, with his elbows bent out, clawing at the muck attached to his head and dripping down the length of him.

He shook his head like a wet dog. In truth, it sort of resembled one of those St.

Bernard dogs that shake their head and slimy spit flies all over the room.

Only this time, it wasn't slimy spit.

It was much, MUCH more disgusting!

Bits of slop and slime sprayed off of him, as he shook his head.

Then he flung more goo, far and wide, as he grabbed chunks of it out of his hair, whipped his arms straight out to the side and flung his hands with fingers splayed to try and dislodge the stuff.

He frantically wiped at his neck trying to keep some of the gross guck from sliding inside of his collar and down into his shirt.

"Oh gross."

"Sick!"

"Did you see that?"

"HA! Had that one coming didn't you Jimmy-O?"

"Ah man, don't touch me with that."

Clearly this little catastrophe had been witnessed by half of the kids in the cafeteria. The comments, hoots, howls, and laughter rocked the place.

Scoop, fling, splat!

Jimmy continued to no avail in dislodging as much of the garbage as possible.

"Way to go Jimmy!"

"You go boy."

"Nasty!"

Viva le Resistance!

"Sorry," Laurie and I giggled in unison.

The comments followed us as we made it the rest of the way out of the cafeteria hallway, through the doorway, and into the sunshine.

Cara was waiting for us as we stepped up into the open courtyard.

"What happened?" She asked curiously trying to peer over our shoulders.

"Sounds like a fight or something."

We quickly described the hilarious scene to her. Cara began giggling.

Cara sounds like a chipmunk when she giggles. It is quite infectious. Even if we hadn't already been giggling over Jimmy's misfortune, we would be giggling now.

Her face turned beet red and she started to emit periodic snorts into the giggles.

We all started walking towards the front of the school, where we usually spend the rest of our lunch hour, when it's nice outside.

Our laughter started to fade and the topic turned to what we were planning on wearing tonight to the dance.

Wardrobe is, after all, a very serious matter.

Laurie and I debated various outfits.

Cara lost interest in the conversation and began to entertain herself.

Viva le Resistance!

She more or less jogged around us with her hands tucked up to her chest, head bobbing up and down the whole time chanting repeatedly, "Viva le resistance."

Why you might ask?

Viva le Resistance!

Good question.

To try and explain Cara, is like trying to explain why a crackling fire hypnotizes you and looking away, at least for a brief moment, is almost impossible.

It just does, and she just is.

That's that.

As we rounded the corner of the building, the front seating area came into view.

Normally, this area is a haven for those of us not under the protective umbrella of the cliquey's or bagmen. It is usually a cornucopia of kids trying to enjoy the brief freedom before the bell rings, signaling the return to class.

Today, however, something wasn't right.

The cliquey's were in a circle around someone and the bagmen appeared to be nervously pacing behind them.

NOT good.

This is not the usual grazing ground of the cliquey's and bagmen. There are, after all, almost no windows, mirrors, or other shiny surfaces on which to view their own beautiousness.

Why then, are the bagmen sheepishly milling around behind the great ones?

Why have they strayed to our corner of the world?

Viva le Resistance!

Who have they ensnared and what are they doing to the poor soul?

Where have the rest of the kids gone, who would be reading, chatting, walking, or otherwise entertaining themselves in the area on any other given day?

When would this madness end?!

Okay, that might be a bit much…I get carried away.

Cara stops dead in her tracks.

Even in Cara's oblivious world, she senses that something is amiss.

Her pink cheeks, which were just suffused in color from the hilarity of Jimmy's misfortune, followed by her rousing rendition of the French fight song, or whatever it was she was doing, are suddenly devoid of color.

Cara herself was once trapped by the cliquey's.

For no apparent reason, other than their own entertainment, the cliquey's will target a person and then torture them until the poor kid cries, intervention occurs by a teacher or the bell rings. If the interruption occurs before the crying begins, the torture is usually resumed at another place and time.

Part of the horror for the recipient is the trepidation. You never know when and you never know how, but know this, they will be back!

Viva le Resistance!

Poor Cara.

She was alone in the bathroom, minding her own business, and doing her own business, on that fateful day.

Why the cliquey's chose Cara that day.....no one will ever know.

They are random in their attack and they are tenacious in the pursuit of a victim.

Cara was in the bathroom when I walked in.

She had her back to the wall to the left of the three stalls. Katie was facing her, hands on her hips, leaning slightly towards Cara, away from me.

Viva le Resistance!

I could only see her back, but judging by her posture I knew something was up.

Julie was standing to the right side of Cara and I definitely had a clear view of her face. She was positively sneering at Cara. Two other cliquey's were standing near the door, but they didn't appear to be as actively involved. They were acting as lookout duty and moral support.

I tried to glance around Katie to see Cara's face. Julie shoved Katie in the arm and nodded towards me.

Katie turned around and said, "Can we help you?" She said it in a snide clipped tone, never taking her hands off of her hips.

Viva le Resistance!

In that instant I could see Cara's face plainly. She looked just like I imagine a baby deer might look, if a mountain lion were standing over the top of it.

I stood mute for a few seconds.

Two other girls started into the bathroom, looked around, and quickly ducked back out. Nobody but nobody knowingly takes on the cliquey's.

Viva le Resistance!

Chapter Thirteen

No one said a word.

I nervously cleared my throat and tried again to get a glimpse of Cara's face.

Katie rocked her weight onto her right leg, bending her left leg, and dropped her left arm to her side.

Julie quickly stepped in front of Cara, blocking my view.

Both had their eyebrows raised and stared at me daring me to say something, I could feel the other two cliquey's circling in behind, between me and the door.

Viva le Resistance!

The little hairs on the back of my neck
stood up.

My mind raced.

Options, THINK, what are my options?

Clearly, I couldn't leave Cara alone.

Obviously no one else was going to
help.

Think….

"Well….." Katie intoned, tapping her
left foot in irritation.

My only hope was something my dad
once said to me.

"Honey, if you can't beat 'em, convince
'em you're crazy."

155

Viva le Resistance!

Odd advice from a father to a daughter, I always thought, but...

I reached over, grabbed the tall trashcan I'd once stored the bagmen's Phat Face 20 book bags in.

I YANKED it over, with all of my might, while simultaneously yelling at the top of my lungs, "Why yes you can help me and DO we have a PROBLEM NOW!!!"

Viva le Resistance!

The trash can CRASHED to the floor
and then rolled noisily across the bathroom,
coming to a stop, bumping against Katie's foot.

She glanced down in surprise and
quickly back up at me.

The adrenaline began to flow and I
actually felt more powerful.

I turned and gave the cliquey's behind
me what I hoped was a very menacing look
and then took a step closer to Katie and Julie.

"You'd best step AWAY from Cara and
walk your happy selves out that door or WE
are going to have some SERIOUS issues."

157

Viva le Resistance!

I threw another glaring look over my
shoulder at the two cliquey's now looking at
each other with worry.

Clearly this was a glitch in their plans.

I stepped over the trashcan, with a
deliberate motion, never taking my eyes from
Katie's.

I watched as the looks flitted quickly
across her face,
irritation, surprise, consternation, uncertainty,
replaced with bored bravado.

Katie clearly didn't believe that I would
ever follow through with my interruption to her
fun. She was not to be bothered by the likes of
me.

Viva le Resistance!

"Girls," she said, "Why don't you help little Annie here out of the bathroom?"

I whirled and gave them my most withering stare.

"Uh, we gotta get to class," they stammered and dashed to the hallway.

I leaned into Katie, until my face was mere inches from her face.

Come on courage, don't fail me now!

Viva le Resistance!

Viva le Resistance!

In a low clipped tone I bit out, "Step away from Cara you insufficient piece of humanity.

You take your annoying, nasty little self right out with your annoying, nasty little friends, or you stick around for awhile."

I calmly pushed my finger into her forehead and gave the most gentle, little push.

Her head rocked backward, ever so slightly.

Her eyes widened.

"Do you REALLY want to see ME get angry?" I said.

Nope!

She didn't.

Viva le Resistance!

Out the door they scurried like rats on a burning ship!

Thank goodness, because just then my strength left me, and my legs began quivering.

I sagged shakily against the wall.

What was I thinking?!

I've never been in a heated argument before (outside of my sister and brother), let ALONE a fight!

What if they'd called my bluff?!

Holy cow!

What was I thinking?!

As I continued to hyperventilate and consider how bad things could have gotten, I looked over to Cara.

Viva le Resistance!

She was curled in a ball, slumped on the floor.

The worries I had for myself vanished, only to be replaced by a surge of protectiveness and concern for her.

"Are you okay?" I asked gently.

No response, but her shoulders were heaving up and down.

Oh no, she's crying!

"Cara," I tried again touching her shoulder, "Are you okay?"

No response.

"Do you want me to get someone?" I pleaded.

What do I do now?

Viva le Resistance!

Her shoulders began heaving up and down more violently.

"Cara…"

She looked up at me. The tears I expected were coursing down her cheeks, but something that I had not expected was happening.

She was LAUGHING!

The tears were from her LAUGHING. She was laughing so hard, the tears were streaking down her face, and she could barely breathe.

"Annie," she struggled to get out, "Annie….(several deep gulping breaths) that..was…so…AWESOME!"

164

Viva le Resistance!

I sat back in stunned silence.

"Your nasty little selves," she gulped, "where on earth did you come up with that?" She finished with a large, unladylike snort.

"Wh-what?" I stuttered.

"Did you see their faces?" she blurted, while wiping her nose across her sleeve.

"I thought Katie was going to have kittens!" She bellowed.

My stunned silence continued, as I tried to grasp what was happening.

Suddenly it hit me.

I had stood up to the cliquey's, and survived, and was now sitting on the bathroom floor with a crazy person, cackling and snorting and giggling uncontrollably.

I, too, began to see the humor in the situation.

"Did you see me throw that trash can?" I grinned at her.

"(Hiccup) Yup! Hoo hoo, it was classic! I wasn't sure if you'd lost it or not. I'm pretty sure Julie wet herself a little when it crashed into the wall!" Cara howled, while rocking back and forth, hugging her sides.

I stared straight forward and began to smile.

Yeah, if you can't beat em,' convince em' you're crazy.

Viva le Resistance!

Thanks dad!

I struggled to my feet, and then reached to pull the convulsing Cara to her feet as well. She staggered as she tried to take the first couple of steps, still racked with spasms of hilarity.

As we struggled towards the bathroom door, straightening our clothes, and glancing towards the mirrors on the far wall to smooth our hair into some semblance of normalcy, Cara whirled towards me.

Cara wrapped her arms around me and yelled, "Viva le resistance!"

She was out the door before I could blink!

Viva le Resistance!

Cara is so weird.

Chapter Fourteen

Between the cliquey's feet, we could see the bottom of a pair of shoes.

From our vantage point, we couldn't see if it was a male or female they were after. The cliquey's weren't discriminating in their selection of prey.

The bagmen, milling around behind them, looked somewhat uncomfortable and giggled nervously amongst themselves.

Laurie placed her hand on my arm and said, "Let's get out of here."

I turned to go with her, but was distracted by what sounded like muffled sobs coming from the direction of the shoes.

If they had gotten tears, why had they not backed off, I wondered.

"No," I said to Laurie apologetically, "I have to see what's going on."

The soles of the shoes looked frighteningly familiar. There were purple letters, spelling L-E-E, on those soles, as in *Lee*.

L-E-E, as in Lee, my little sister.

My heart beat faster and my paced quickened.

Viva le Resistance!

Pansy or no, I was not walking away from this one.

I shoved my way through the bagmen. I thought I saw Sam glance at me apologetically.

Why was he here?

Why was he not helping?

Sam is the defender of the underdog.

Isn't he?

He's always come to the defense of kids getting picked on, like Kylie when Jimmy was being such a jerk on the bus.

He is my hero, my love, my big goofy white knight.

Isn't he?

Viva le Resistance!

I shoved Julie and Katie apart and looked down upon Corey, my little sister's best friend. She is wearing Lee's shoes and she is crying.

She is sitting in the dirt with the cliquey's hovering over her and she is CRYING.

My blood begins to boil.

Katie and Corey are THREE years younger than us! They are only in FIFTH GRADE for goodness sake! That's an all time low, even for the cliquey's!

I looked to find Sam but he averted his eyes and kicked at the dirt beneath his feet sheepishly. Lane giggled nervously and turned away.

Disillusioned with my beloved and horrified at the spectacle of Corey's sad little dirt and tear stained face, I turn on the cliquey's. In my peripheral vision I see Lee struggling to keep from crying as well.

I ... SEE ... RED.

With a last glance at Sam to see if he might actually try to help (he didn't), I slowly advance towards Katie.

As I contemplate whether to launch myself at her face or her stomach first, I hear, "Ka- ahem- Katie."

Viva le Resistance!

In a squeaky-voice-is-changing-and-I'm nervous tone, "Katie, you guys need to leave her alone!"

I look around to Sam glad that he'd finally decided to redeem himself, but Sam was also looking around with a surprised expression, as were all of the bagmen and cliquey's.

Actually, pretty much everyone in earshot was doing the same.

Patrick stepped forward, as the crowd parted.

Viva le Resistance!

"You guys need to just back off and leave her alone," he said in a stronger tone.

Patrick?

Patrick alone stood up to the bagmen AND cliquey's?

Whoa.

Viva le Resistance!

Patrick is in 7th grade. He lives on a farm 5 miles south of ours. He is about my height, with blond hair and blue eyes. Patrick has really big glasses and he has a nervous habit of using his right pointer finger to push them up by the bridge.

Patrick is very shy.

I only remember him talking once before.

We were in third grade. Actually I was in third grade and Patrick was in second grade. A group of us would gather at recess and play together. We often played "house" in which we had roles we assumed. One day when I was the "mother," Patrick walked up. He stood very quietly as we all played.

The next day he did the same.

And the next…

And the next..

Eventually Patrick worked up the courage to talk to me.

He asked, "Can I play with you guys?"

When he asked his head was bent down looking at his feet. He was shuffling them around in the dirt, rather than look at me.

I said, "Sure."

At my response he glanced up through his white-blond wavy bangs and smiled timidly.

177

I said, "But we already have a brother, sister, mother, father, aunt, two uncles, a dog, and two cats.

So….if you want to play with us you'll have to be my decoration."

"Okay," he softly replied, "What do I have to do?"

"You have to be decoration. You know…a decoration. Like a picture on the wall," I explained.

"Oh," he said looking confused.

I demonstrated. I took Patrick by the shoulders and pretended to "lift him up." I then moved him and "placed" him on the imaginary wall.

"There. You are now our decoration. No moving around. You are a pretty to look at," I finished with a flourish of my hand in a Vana-esque manner, "Perfect!"

For the next several weeks Patrick would follow us out to play, assuming his role as our decoration, never moving from the spot or talking. He would have probably continued, but our group moved on to a new pastime.

Patrick never complained. He never asked for a 'new position' in the family. He was just content to be included in some small way.

Here was quiet, shy, unassuming little Patrick taking on the establishment!

He was rocking the boat on behalf of my sister's little friend.

The bagmen froze tableau-like.

The cliquey's, at first, appeared not to hear. They remained in their threatening stance, over the now sobbing Corey.

Katie's brows wrinkled into a puzzled look. She stood with arms akimbo and her face scrunched in annoyance. Katie turned slightly toward Julie and cocked her head to the side in a, "WHAT the," manner.

Julie and the other cliquey's raised their shoulders with hands out and up in a, "Heck if I know," gesture glancing back and forth at each other with similar raised eyebrow expressions.

The cliquey's turned, en masse, towards little Patrick. The gathered masses witnessing the event stood still and silent.

A collective breath was drawn.

Chapter Fifteen

"WHAT did YOU say to ME?" Katie spat out slowly while leaning towards Patrick with her hands on her hips.

Actually, all of the cliquey's assumed the aggressive stance of Her-Royal-Nastiness.

The Bagmen slowly walk forward, closing ranks around Patrick. Even my Sam joins in the posturing. The tension rises in everyone witnessing the ghastly scene unfolding.

No Sam!

Not you!

Viva le Resistance!

How COULD you?!

Sam's eyes met mine and he gave me what looked like an apologetic shrug, but still he maintained his position.

My mind raced as Patrick straightened his back, and with his right pointer finger shakily pushed his glasses up the bridge of his nose. His prescription is strong enough that the result was the magnification of his scared dark blue eyes.

Dark blue eyes, I'd never noticed.

"I SAID," he began with his voice still shaking, "Katie, you guys need to leave her alone."

"And if we don't?" she menaced.

Viva le Resistance!

As the exchange took place, a subtle change occurred in the surrounding crowd. A milling about was occurring. I moved up behind Patrick. Laurie stood to my left. Cara defiantly sidled up on my right, whispering quietly, "Viva le Resistance."

What is with her?

We were not the only ones challenging the great ones. To my surprise, I looked up to see kids meandering over to stand behind Patrick as well. Lots of kids joined us. Lots and lots of kids, some I didn't even recognize joined in support.

As Patrick cleared his throat to answer, the bell rang.

Viva le Resistance!

Patrick's face clearly registered a look of relief at the distraction, but he never relaxed his posture. He continued to stare into Katie's eyes, as she glared back at him.

With a, "Hmmph, that's what I THOUGHT!" She and her herd whirled, with gorgeous manes fanning out behind them, and stalked back towards the school. The Bagmen followed. Sam, again, glanced towards me and quickly away.

Patrick kindly reached a hand down to a sniffling Corey.

She reached up to his with unabashed adoration clearly written all over her face.

"Thank you." She beamed up at him as he helped her to her feet.

Lee rushed forward both hands out in supplication.

"Thank you! Thank you so much!" she gushed to Patrick. In her angst, she threw her arms around my waist and buried her head against my chest. She was openly crying now. Hugging her, I grinned at Patrick. He smiled sweetly back at me and Lee.

"No prob-lem," his voice squeaked a little on the last syllable. He pushed his glasses up the bridge of his nose with his right pointer finger (which was no longer shaking I noticed.)

Viva le Resistance!

"I can't stand to see a little kid getting picked on," he said, putting his arm around Corey's shoulder.

"I know exactly what you mean," I replied, as I looked down at Lee, "It's one thing for Lee and I to go at it at home, but for a group to scare a little kid….that's just not right." I gave Lee's shoulders a squeeze.

Looking down at her, I said, "This doesn't change anything you know. You are still the biggest pain."

Grabbing Corey by the hand and turning away, she laughed, "I know, Cakie Goodie Choo-Choo!"

"Doggie Daddie Ralph!" I grinned.

Viva le Resistance!

Quizzically, Patrick looked at me as we
started to walk back with the rest of the
students, in response to the bell. Sheepishly, I
looked around to see who might overhear our
conversation. Laurie and Cara were laughingly
walking up ahead of us now, oblivious to our
discussion. No one else appeared to be the
least bit interested.

Rolling my eyes, I began, "You see, Lee
and I shared a room when we were younger.
We had twin beds with a foot or so of space
between the two. Every night my mom would
come down to read to us. She sat in her
threadbare, worn out, old blue robe on my bed,
hunched over the book. When she was done,

188

she would kiss each of us and say, 'Good night. Sweet dreams. I love you.'"

Patrick grinned.

"I know, I know, pretty embarrassing. Don't worry, it gets worse!" I giggled, looking around again to ensure that no one else would hear of my humiliation.

"When Lee was about five, she decided we should say it to each other too, but neither of us could actually bring our self to say it....sooooooo..." I glanced up at him to see if he was laughing at me yet.

He wasn't.

I continued, "We sort of came up with code words for it."

189

Viva le Resistance!

He laughed at that, "What do you mean?"

His eyes are REALLY dark blue.

"'Cakie, Goodie, Choo-Choo' is code for 'Goodnight. Sweet dreams. I love you.' And 'Doggie Daddie Ralph,' is code for 'Goodnight. I love you too.'" I finished, feeling my face burning red.

He stopped, looked me in the eye, and said, "I gotta get to class."

Interesting segue.

"Okaaaay?" I stammered at his retreating back.

Odd.

Viva le Resistance!

"What was that about?" Cara asked, seeing my confused look at Patrick's abrupt departure.

"I'm not exactly sure," I reply with my head tipped slightly to the side, and my right eyebrow raised, still watching his retreating figure down the hallway.

Kids were bumping and pushing their way through the hallway and we were being jostled about.

"Sure about what?" Laurie asked walking up beside us.

"See ya!" Cara tossed back over her shoulder as she bounded off.

Viva le Resistance!

"Just a really weird conversation I had with Patrick. He sort of walked away in the middle of it," I told Laurie as she walked along beside me.

Viva le Resistance!

Leaning to look around me, Laurie said, "Patrick was great wasn't he?"

"Mmm-hmm," I responded bemusedly.

I felt a hand at my elbow.

"Annie?" Sam said quietly, "Can I talk to you?"

Sam's face looked red. He kept his face down and glanced up at me with his eyes.

Those beautiful blue eyes.

I looked around, asking with derision, "So. Where are the rest of your *people*?"

Sam grimaced slightly.

"That's what I want to talk to you about," he replied, staring imploringly into my eyes.

Viva le Resistance!

"Sam," Julie's voice broke in, "Let's go. Katie and Ron are waiting."

"Yes Sam," I said, mimicking Julie's voice, "Katie and Ron are waiting."

I whirled and stalked off, leaving Sam and Julie standing together in the hallway. I fled to the restroom, leaning my head against the cool tile wall.

Hopefully that tile wall had been cleaned recently.

The events of the past hour were playing in my head. Sam told me he wasn't going with Julie. He told me he wasn't *in* to her.

But Tori said that Sam IS going with Julie. Sam is the champion of the underdog, and yet he'd let Katie and her posse terrorize Corey, without saying a word.

What is going on?

My heart is breaking.

There MUST be an explanation.

Tori must have heard wrong.

That's it!

Tori misunderstood. Tori must have heard Ron ASKING Sam if he wanted to go with Julie and ASSUMED he had agreed.

THAT had to be IT!

And Sam wasn't just WATCHING Katie torture Corey, he was merely considering the best way to intervene.

Yes, that HAD to be it. If Patrick hadn't been quicker, Sam would have JUMPED to Corey's defense.

I knew it! My Sam doesn't want JULIE and he CERTAINLY wouldn't have just stood by without helping.

Whew.

How could I have EVER doubted my beloved?

The birds are singing again!

I turned into the office, intending to call my mom about the detention after school.

"Mr. Shelpick, may I use the phone to call my mom?" I asked.

"Is it an e-mer-gency?" he drawled out nasally.

"No Mr. Shelpick, Mr. Harlin said that we all have to stay after school tonight with him and Mr. Johns," I replied.

"Oooooh, you are in *THAT* class," he said, with extra nasally emphasis on *THAT*.

"Unfortunately," I said, rolling my eyes and nodding my head.

Viva le Resistance!

"Make it quick," he warned, handing me the phone.

Chapter Sixteen

Ring

Ring

"Hello."

"Hi Mom."

Silence.

"Mom?"

"What's wrong."

"Wellllllllll," I began.

Briefly, I explained what had happened in Mr. Harlin's classroom, with extra emphasis on the fact that I was completely innocent.

Viva le Resistance!

There I was, innocently singing my heart out, trying my very best to be a good musical student, when my dastardly classmates had so abused poor Mr. Harlin.

Tragic.

It was just awful.

What WAS I to do?

Mr. Shelpick looked up at me shaking his head and rolling his eyes in a yeah-right-she'll-really-believe-THAT-one sort of way.

"MMM-HHMM," she muttered loudly, with a suspiciously facetious tone.

How RUDE!

"Young lady," she began.

Viva le Resistance!

Uh-oh. Young-lady-ing me is almost as bad as middle naming me.

"I have been to that school TWICE today. Your brother forgot his geometry book and assignment and your sister forgot her gym shorts. Exactly how many times do you kids expect me to drive in today?" She finished with exasperation.

"I guess three times!" I lilt, thinking a little humor will lighten the mood!

Wrong.

"Annie. I am NOT driving to school three times today. I drove in twice and that is TWICE too many for one day. Do you understand me?" Mom snapped.

Yikes.

"You, Annie Kay, are going to call your *FATHER*. You are going to call your father and tell HIM that you need a ride. You tell HIM that YOU got in trouble and HE needs to come pick you up," she drawled in what seemed a suspiciously pleasant tone.

Ack! Young-lady-ed AND middle-named! Not good at all!

"In FACT," her tone rising, "I will call him FOR you. Have a nice day," followed by a distinct click!

She hung up on me!

Of all the nerve!

Viva le Resistance!

Detention wasn't too bad. I've never
actually HAD a detention before so I was kind
of excited!

It was a bit of a letdown actually.

I expected a darkened basement room,
with large cobweb strings hanging from
exposed light bulbs. Most of the light bulbs
would, of course, be burned out. One in the
back would be flickering annoyingly,
reminiscent of an old black and white
Frankenstein film.

There would be old wooden desks, with
carvings made by countless juvenile
delinquents, caged over the long dreary years.
Seated sparsely, would be thug-like students in

leather jackets with chains and buckles, hunched over these scarred desks.

They would have long, straggly hair falling over their eyes, as they sneered up at my intrusion, only to go back to the work of carving, with pen-knives clutched tightly in meaty fists.

Instead, Sam and Lane sat in the front row playing paper football. Laurie sat near the back of the room waving brightly at me and pointing at the chair next to her. The rest of the class was filled with students from music. Mr. Johns sat at the front of the room, joking with Mr. Nelson. Mr. Harlin was no where to be found.

Poor guy, he probably still hadn't recovered.

Mr. Nelson piped up, "Settle down. Sounds like you guys gave Mr. Harlin a rough time. Not cool. Get out any work you may have and begin. If you don't have anything to work on, sit quietly. You are with me until the big hand is on the ten."

With a little grumbling, we all pretty much did what Mr. Nelson said.

We like Mr. Nelson.

When dad came to pick me up, I expected the worst. Well, not really. Mom likes to think she's "sicking dad on us" when really, he just grins or rolls his eyes and tells us to knock it off.

When we were little and REALLY messed up, mom used to swat us with a fly swatter. We would writhe and howl and beg for mercy, but it really didn't hurt at all. It was a racket we had going. She thought she was really punishing us, and we knew we were really getting away with something.

It was win win.

It was win win, until dad saw her in action with the fly swatter, that is. He started laughing and asked why she bothered. Why not just use a feather duster and really show us, he joked. She grabbed the fly swatter and chased him around the kitchen, smacking him with it. He laughed and ducked as she smacked at him.

Finally, he snatched it from her and began chasing her around the kitchen smacking at her.

Mom wasn't laughing.

After that, when a good swatting was deserved, mom whipped off her SHOE! They were slip-on shoes so easy access for meting out discipline.

The shoe DID hurt!

The avoidance of the shoe, for me, was imperative. I don't like pain. Once my mom took umbrage with a water fight my brother and I got into. He sprayed me with the hose repeatedly then ran into the house for safety.

Believing vengeance more important than my mother's impending wrath, I filled a five-gallon bucket up with that same hose. I staggered with the weight of the bucket and water slopping noisily over the edge and onto my shoe.

I heaved the bucket up with both hands, waddled with it suspended precariously between my legs, sloshing my shoes with each swaying footstep. Arriving at the back door, I sat the bucket down, still straddling it. I opened the screen door and propped it with my back.

Viva le Resistance!

Leaning over the bucket, I reached in with my right hand and turned the doorknob. The door yawned open to the right, bumping the wall. I lifted the bucket with both hands, taking straddling steps around it.

Up three steps, I hoisted the bucket, much lighter now as a vast majority of the water had sloshed over the edge onto me, the sidewalk, and now the carpet.

Bent on my mission of revenge, impending danger, in the form of my mother, did not actually occur to me.

My brother was still barricading himself in the bathroom. I lifted the bucket of water, now much more manageable in bulk, and tapped the door with my foot. Thinking himself in the clear, my brother opened the door.

With my left hand holding the bucket handle and my right hand on the underside lip of the bucket, I HEAVED the contents at him. The freezing liquid deluge caught him full in the face and chest!

He GASPED!

Awesome!

He never saw it coming!

Unfortunately, my mother happened to be standing behind me when I launched my nefarious attack!

Viva le Resistance!

She didn't see the brilliance of my
diabolical scheme.
She couldn't appreciate the utter delight in a
delicious deliverance of avengement.

She saw a bathroom, waterlogged by her
daughter. She saw her son standing, fully
clothed, and soaked to the bone.

My mom really has no sense of humor.
UH-OH!

Mom snakes her left arm out snatching
me up by the arm, while simultaneously
whipping her shoe off her right foot. She
raises the shoe ....

Let the beating begin!

Chapter Seventeen

Did I mention that my mom is not a big woman?

I dropped to the floor, as my mom took the first swipe!

MISSED!

Ha *HA!*

With mom holding my left arm, I scooted my feet out as FAR away from her swinging arm as possible. I ran in circles around her, keeping my feet and, therefore, my hind end out of range. Round and round I went, with her swinging, we must have looked like a demented merry-go-round of sorts.

We both ended up dizzy and laughing.

She never did land an actual swat!

I did, however, end up having to clean up the bathroom by myself.

Not fair I tell you, not fair at all!

My dad pulled up to the curb with a big wave and a smile.

My dad is the most handsome dad in the world. He has dark hair parted to the side. Dad's eyes are green and he has laugh lines etched deeply into his temples.

Viva le Resistance!

Viva le Resistance!

Dad is smiling at me as I pull open the door of his truck and swing my way inside. Dad drives a big Ford F-250 with oversized tires. I have to sort of jump towards the handle over the passenger door. I grasp it with both hands, luckily catching hold of it on my first try!

That is not always the case!

Grasping the handle tightly, I heave my left leg high into the front seat area, while simultaneously using the overhead handle for momentum; I hoist my bottom into the seat swinging my right leg in behind me. This acrobatic feat completed, and face slightly reddened from exertion, I turn to my father.

215

"So," he asked laconically, "how's things?"

Sheepishly, I glance sideways at him, "Been better."

"Your mom is pretty irritated with you," Dad grinned.

"Yeah huh?" I tried to sound as innocent as possible.

"She told me to, 'Go and pick up YOUR daughter.'" He laughed outright.

"She middle-named me AND called me young lady," I giggled, "I KNEW I was in trouble THEN!"

We rode home chatting amicably about our day.

Viva le Resistance!

Pulling into the driveway, however, we both changed our outwardly demeanor appropriately. Dad pulled a face, looking at once irritated and exasperated. I, accordingly, assumed a dejected and chastised expression.

Mom hovered at the door, with hands on hips. She had her mouth pursed, eyes squinty, and her right eyebrow raised. Mom looked intently at both of us, boring into our expressions for validation of authenticity I suspect.

I think Mom does suspect that Dad isn't really as hard on us as she is wanting. I sometimes wonder if it is a game she plays, knowing full well what machinations we are employing to circumvent her system!

It is probably part of her diabolical plot to control our very existence!

My Mom is smart that way!

Dad glares down at my head, while I keep my chin tucked and head down.

With the eyebrow still raised, she glances back and forth between Dad and me.

"Taken care of?" she asks my father simply.

"Done," he replies with an irritated sounding growl.

"Well?" She next directs to me.

218

Viva le Resistance!

"Sorry Mom," I mumble, still staring at the floor.

Silence

With a whirl she says, "Good, dinner will be ready in an hour. You both best get cleaned up!"

The happy lilt was back in her tone and she took to flouncing around the kitchen again.

My Mom is really quite easily distracted from her temper. She is about my height, with dark brown hair. Her eyes, like mine, are so dark; it is difficult to discern the pupil from the iris. Mom has laugh lines like Dad, but they are more delicate. She has very pale, almost ivory, skin. My Mom, although usually forced

219

to be the disciplinarian in the family for OBVIOUS reasons, is very kind and compassionate.

Heading for the basement and my room, I thump loudly down the stairs. At the bottom of our stairs is an unfinished room. It is gray brick with a cold, uncarpeted cement floor and a sump pump hole in the corner.

The sump pump hole has been a problem over the years.

You see, my sister has an affinity for gerbils. Lee buys the gerbil, names the gerbil, falls in love with the gerbil, and plays with the gerbil.

Viva le Resistance!

Like all responsible gerbil-owners, Lee has researched how to care for her gerbil.

The books, pet storeowners, and various other gerbil-friendly-information-centers, suggest that gerbils enjoy a romp in a gerbil mobile. Lee's gerbil mobile is a clear ball with air holes designed for the gerbil to cruise around the house, unable to escape, but given a freedom not afforded by the running wheel in the cage.

Viva le Resistance!

Viva le Resistance!

Happily, the gerbil gallivants about our home, peeking in corners and crevices, driving our cat, Chuck, insane.

Until....the gerbil finds out that it is owned by Lee, at which time the gerbils have, one-by-one, headed for the stairs, dived headlong down the stairs, shaken their little gerbil-heads to clear the disorientation, and with the determination of a kamikaze pilot, plunged headlong into the sump-pump hole!

We've tried baby-gates for the stairs, we've tried putting up barricades to the sump pump hole, and we've even tried limiting the gerbil to Lee's room ONLY when out and about in the gerbil-mobile.

To no avail, the gerbils invariably feel the need to commit suicide, at the notion of being owned by Lee.

This is what my brother and I tell her anyway.

It's always nice when siblings can be caring and supporting of one another in such a way.

Usually, the gerbil-suicide is followed by a funeral, with a proper burial in a checkbook box coffin designed by Lee. After a brief period of mourning, Lee heads back to the pet store to try again.

The unfinished room, besides being a deathtrap for gerbils, is haunted. Maybe not haunted in the traditional sense that might include a ghost or other apparition; however, in my mind it is haunted nevertheless. Since moving to this house as a little girl, I've always been frightened by the dark, cold, slightly sinister feel of the unfinished basement room.

My method for avoidance is and has always been, to dart quickly and loudly down the stairs, pausing breathlessly at the bottom stair. I reach slowly around the partition wall and grope blindly for the light switch. I fling on the lights for both the unfinished room and the adjacent family room. Finally, I make a mad dash for my bedroom, past my brother's bedroom, simultaneously flooding my own room with light and slamming my door shut.

Today is no different!

In my room and slightly out of breath, I bend over with hands on my knees. After a few quick breaths, I straighten up, looking at my closet.

What to wear.

What to wear.

Hmmmmm.

I should have brought the phone with me to call Laurie.

"Kids!" Yelling down the stairs, Mom draws out the word and it sounds more like kiids, "It's time to eat." Eat is also drawn out and sounds like ea-eat.

Over Rick's noisy chewing, Mom's muffled etiquette critiques involving closing his mouth when he chews, and the usual, "Please pass the," and other typical table commotion, Lee blathered on about her day. She sat up straighter and with a look of simple adoration, told of Patrick's daring bravery.

Without looking up, and between bites, my dad paused with a food-ladened fork, "I always like that Patrick. He seems like a good kid."

Curiously I looked up.

"You know Patrick?" I asked.

227

Chewing in an exaggerated manner, while nodding, Dad swallowed loudly.

"Yeah, good kid. I've seen him over at the coop with Stan," he spit a little food as he replied.

Eewww.

"What was he doing with Stan?" I asked, reaching for another roll and glancing carefully at my Mom to see if she noticed. They aren't still pushing the diet thing since I grew, but I still have some food-issues.

"He works for Stan. Has since he was 11 or 12 I think. Spends every afternoon, weekends, and summers over there at the farm," Dad said.

No wonder I never see him at any games or anything.

Stan is Sam's father.

Dad continued, "Yeah, that kid of his…what is it…Sam? I think. Yeah, Sam isn't much on the chores. Too busy with his friends and his sports I guess. Anyway, that Patrick kid works for them."

Interesting.

I didn't know that Patrick worked for Sam's dad.

With a noisy clattering of plates and chairs scraping away from the table Dad and Rick went in to watch TV. Lee, Mom, and I cleared the table, rinsed the dishes, loaded the dishwasher and wiped off the counters.

"Mom," I said.

"Yeah sweetie," she replied without looking up.

"If you really liked someone, but they did something that wasn't right, would you still like them?" I wondered aloud.

"Well honey," she said, still holding the cloth she'd been using on the stove, "I guess that depends."

I stood still listening intently.

"If it was something that you know wasn't right, and you know THEY know it wasn't right, I'd say you have some thinking to do," she was smiling gently at me.

This was starting to feel like an after school special.

Discomfited, I squirmed a bit, "But, what if it was a misunderstanding? Maybe this person was GOING to do the right thing, but just got …. I don't know….. distracted?"

I remembered Sam's apologetic shrug.

Was it apologetic, or was it really UN-apologetic.

Oh MAN.

"Annie," Mom turned fully towards me holding her left hand with the rag over the sink, squeezed all of the excess soapy water out, and dropped it across the sink partition, "I think you know the answer. Right is right. Wrong is wrong. I'm not sure what we are talking about here, but I do know that YOU know."

What?!

My mom can be a bit convoluted at times!

With a start I said, "Guess I'd better be getting ready! Laurie's mom is picking me up at 6:45."

Chapter Eighteen

At exactly 7:00, Laurie and I stepped into the gym. Of course, the gym was just a gym, but with the music playing in the background and the lights low, if you squint up your eyes and slightly closed one of them...

Nah, it is still just a gym.

The music was loud, the beat pulsed through the floor, and I could feel it through my shoes. Almost immediately, Keith strolled over and asked Laurie to dance.

Keith had a nice, bright, white bandage across his chin.

233

Viva le Resistance!

"Ouch," I grimaced empathetically, "That looks like it hurt!"

"Three stitches," he nodded, touching his chin gingerly.

"EEESH," I wrinkled my nose, "Sorry I couldn't hold you up! I really tried!"

"No worries," he winked, leading Laurie to dance.

They make a pretty cute couple. He is tall with that dark straight-straight hair and she is fair with that short wavy hair.

Wonder if Lane will mind.

Works for me!

Cara jigged her way over to me. She had taken her long braids out for the occasion and pushed a colorful headband high on her head. Her long wavy black hair floated around her like a cloud, reaching almost to her waist.

For a goof, Cara is quite lovely when she cleans up!

"Seen Sam?" She begins with little provocation.

"Nooooo…" I draw the word out while raising my eyebrows and tilting my head slightly to the side, "Why?" I'm almost afraid to ask.

"Just wondering," she jigs away leaving me with a quizzical expression staring after her.

Odd girl.

Viva le Resistance!

Looking around I see most of 7th and 8th grade class. The usual groups are segregating themselves to their various corners. The bagmen and cliquey's are swarming around the table with cookies and punch.

Katie is looking breathtaking, in an obviously new outfit, and her hair pulled up tightly. She clearly had her hair professionally coiffed as it was designed to look both elegant and carefree, with perfect tendrils kissing her temples and nape.

I hope she gets head lice again.

I spot Sam tucked in behind Lane and Ron. Nonchalantly, I glance towards him as I pretend to stroll casually by.

He smiles at me.

I continue on my fictitious path until I am standing at the far side of the gym, next to the bleachers.

On the bleachers sit the shy kids. These are the kids that are almost nonentities `socially. I've never really understood why they bother to attend dances. They sit together, almost as if with assigned seating arrangements.

I've never actually been to a dance that these same kids weren't sitting in the same seats watching the dancers with a feigned lack of interest.

Viva le Resistance!

At the Christmas dance last December, I took a piece of mistletoe from the main entrance. I went to the bleachers attendees and held it over each one of them giving them a quick peck on the cheek with a, "Merry Christmas." Then I asked each to dance. Only three took me up on my request. Two looked a little green and one excused himself to the restroom rather quickly!

Viva le Resistance!

Ah well, such is life!

Viva le Resistance!

Ruminating fondly, I felt a slight tug on my sleeve. Looking up I saw the beautiful dark blue eyes of Patrick staring down at me.

Patrick sits in the bleachers with these guys?

"Last time you asked me to dance, I was too embarrassed," he gazed down at me.

I asked him to dance?

"But I really enjoyed the kiss," his eyes sparkled.

The kiss?!

He was at the Christmas dance?

Why don't I remember?!

Sheesh!

Viva le Resistance!

"Would you care to dance?" he asked, reaching his right hand out to me with his palm up.

"Sure," I reply, placing my left hand in his.

We actually spent the next few songs dancing together. They were all slow songs and Patrick really just put his hands lightly on my waist and swayed back and forth. We didn't talk at all, and he only looked in my eyes once, but he did ask me after each song if I'd like to dance the next as well.

The next song had a fast beat. Apparently Patrick isn't up for a fast dance yet.

"Thank you," he murmured quietly and turned to walk back to the bleacher seats. His remained empty as if waiting for his return.

Something is different about him.

Glasses! NO glasses.

"Hey," I started, grabbing his arm lightly, "Where are your glasses?"

"I got contacts today," shyly he bent his head, "What do you think?"

"I think you look GR.." bumped roughly from behind, I whirled around without finishing my statement.

"Oh EX-cuuse me," Katie sneered, "So SORRY."

She giggled to Julie and the others.

"Did I HURT you?" She continued.

"Not at all," I retorted, "I think with all of that air in your head, it makes you more bouncy." Grinning I walked off towards Laurie.

From behind me I heard, "Now I see why Sam thinks she's stupid."

"Yeah, I heard he told her he wanted her to go to the dance with him so he could stand · her up."

What?!

"That would be so funny."

Too many voices chiming in, I couldn't tell who was saying what.

Viva le Resistance!

Turning, I bumped into someone tall and solid.

Sam!

"Annie," his soft melodious voice whispered, "Do you want to dance?"

Do I!

"Viva le Resistance!" Cara exclaimed bouncing happily by!

"I would love to," I exclaimed looking up into his eyes.

He gently placed his hand on the small of my back, guiding me towards the center of the dance floor. His hand was warm and felt "right," as we strolled together.

Viva le Resistance!

Laurie and Lane were now dancing together. We walked towards them and Sam turned towards me. He gently placed his hands on my hips and I put my arms around his neck. The song was slow. He held me a little closer as the song played.

I glanced over and saw Laurie grinning broadly at us. I gave her thumbs up behind Sam's head. We swayed languidly to the music. I drifted into my own happy little world.

Could life get any better?

Eventually the song ended. Sam kept his hands on my hips and asked if I was enjoying myself.

Oh yeah!

I nodded.

Another song began and we began to sway.

"Sam," I said, softly tipping my head back to see his face.

He stared down into mine, "Yes?"

"THERE you are," a shrill voice from behind me.

"Sam, can I talk to you?" Julie continued.

Great.

Just great!

Sam looked down at me apologetically, "Do you mind?"

Viva le Resistance!

MIND! Are you CRAZY! Of
COURSE I mind!

"Not at all," I shrugged indifferently.

Laurie looked on with concern. She and
Lane were still dancing together. He has been
sweet on her for so long. I think he is
entranced with the moment! She raises her
eyebrows at me with a should-I-come-with-you
look. I shook my head with a little smile.

Let her enjoy her moment.

Walking away, as if it were the most
natural thing in the world to do in the middle
of a song, when your dance partner has been
shanghaied from you, I peeked toward the

bleachers. Sure enough, Patrick was watching me. I grinned at him. He grinned back.

A commotion was stirring at the front of the gym. Sauntering in that general direction, I caught sight of Jimmy. It was a cleaned up, slicked back version of Jimmy, but Jimmy nevertheless.

"Hey drippy!"

"How's it HANGING goo-boy?"

The catcalls began amidst the laughter.

"Whoa, must have scraped the majority of it off, eh?"

"Nasty! I can still smell him from here!"

"Nice going GARBAGE Maaaaan!"

Viva le Resistance!

"Hey yeah, GARBAGE Man!"

"Gar-bage Man, Gar-bage Man, Gar-bage Man...."

Oh dear. The whole gym seemed to shake with the chant that had been taken up by most of the student body. This could be one that stuck for a long, long time, as some nicknames are apt to do. If Jimmy weren't such a slime-ball, I might actually feel sorry for him.

"Cut it out guys," a soft voice said.

Patrick cleared his throat and then spoke out more forcefully, "CUT IT OUT."

Astonished expressions, followed by silence.

Interesting.

Intrigued, I drew closer, "Are you friends with Jimmy?" I asked.

"No," looking down at his feet, Patrick replied, "I just really hate to see people getting picked on. Even people, who kind of deserve it, shouldn't be ganged up on by everyone."

The guy has a point.

Before I can respond, Laurie pulls on my arm. Let's go to the girls' room she says, which is of course code for, "Let's talk."

Chapter Nineteen

"What's going on with you and that Patrick guy?" She asks without preamble.

"What do you mean?" I ask really surprised.

"Lane said that Sam really wants to be with you tonight, but every time he looks up, you are off canoodling with Patrick."

What?!

"I know, she's such a..." Katie and the cliquey's jostle their way into the restroom, and stops short with her comment.

Viva le Resistance!

"Ooooh, so HERE you are," she scoffs, "Look Julie, here is the little boyfriend stealer now."

What?!

"Couldn't find your own boyfriend so you had to steal mine, huh?" Julie leaned in menacingly. Julie was wearing a very low cut shirt and as she leaned toward me with her lip curled. I could see all the way down her blouse!

Oh now that's nice.

I did NOT need to see THAT! I may be scarred for LIFE!

Viva le Resistance!

Laurie spoke up, "She did NOT steal her BOYFRIEND. Sam clearly likes Annie better. He has good taste."

"Oh, now we have Mutt AND Jeff do we?" Katie jeered.

Just as the situation appeared to be REALLY heating up, Mrs. Mark stepped into the restroom, "Ladies, do we have a problem in here?"

She glared back and forth between the cliquey's and where Laurie and I were standing. I don't think Mrs. Mark has ever liked me much, after the aroma-induced ending to the burgeoning friendship between her daughter and me. Come to think of it, I think

Viva le Resistance!

she was none too fond of me even when we WERE friends!

"Girls, you need to be on your way," she announced firmly. Clearly she was going nowhere until we cleared out.

With a final toss of their beautiful hair, the beautiful ones departed. Laurie and I breathed a sigh of relief and, under the watchful stare of Mrs. Mark, left as well.

"I think maybe I need to talk with Sam and find out what's going on," I said to Laurie.

Sam and Lane were waiting for us in the hallway. Lane and Laurie clasped hands and walked purposefully back toward the dance floor.

Viva le Resistance!

Sam and I watched until they were gone.

"MM –hmm," he cleared his throat.

"Can I ask what is going on?" I inquired beseechingly.

"What do you mean?" he replied.

Oh great, passive aggressive or obtuse?!

"Well, I guess I sort of thought you wanted to be here with me tonight," I ventured uncertainly.

"I really do," Sam rushed, "It's just that Katie and Ron sort of invited Julie on my behalf and just assumed they were doing me a favor."

Nice.

Viva le Resistance!

"So do you like her?" cringing on the inside, I waited for the answer.

"Not really, she's kind of pushy," he kicked at an invisible piece of dirt.

"Pushy?" I say, dreading the answer.

"Well," he looked up at me and the quickly back toward the floor, "She sort of kissed me on the way here."

Oh no she didn't!

"Did you want her to kiss you?" I asked.

"No, she just sort of did," he said.

"And....what did you do?" I reply looking directly into his eyes this time.

"What do you mean," he looked confused.

"Did you kiss her back?" I said slowly and deliberately.

"Well… yeah…I didn't want her to feel stupid or anything," Sam expelled a breath.

Mentally banging my head against the wall.

"So, let me get this straight," I said rather heatedly, "YOU wanted to come with ME, but RON and KATIE invited JULIE, so you went along with it! THEN on the way over here, even though you wanted to be with ME, YOU KISSED her BACK because you didn't want her to feel STUPID OR ANYTHING."

"Yeeaahh.." he quietly drawled out.

"Sam," I said in a low voice, "Why didn't you help Corey when they had her surrounded AND crying on the ground at lunch?"

"I didn't want Ron to get mad at me if I said anything to Katie," he refused eye contact.

"Let me guess....you didn't want her to feel STUPID or anything!" I shouted.

"Well......yeah," he agreed.

Oh my GOODNESS! This is NOT happening!

Viva le Resistance!

"Do you see any flaws in your logic?" I demanded.

"Um...what?" he looked confused.

Oh you have GOT to be kidding me!

How could I have NOT seen this side of him?! White knight my foot! He was dense!

What was I THINKING!?

"SA-AM! SA-aaam!" Julie hollered down the hallway, "Sam I need you right this instant."

"Sam, I hope you and Julie are happy together," I stalked back towards the dance.

"Wait Annie," he called, "I really want to work this out with you."

Viva le Resistance!

I kept walking. As I turned to go into the gym, I saw Julie had a possessive death-grip on Sam's arm and was hanging heavily into him. He, however, was looking disconsolately towards me. His eyes pleaded for me to go back.

Yeah right!

Chapter Twenty

Laurie met me at the door.

"What HAPPENED?" she asked expectantly.

Giving her a brief rundown of the interaction, I shook my head. I still couldn't believe it myself. Here I had been utterly infatuated with a guy, who probably couldn't even spell the word! He might even need to look it up in the dictionary if I sprung it on him!

The music seemed too loud now, and the garish decorations no longer looked quaint, they actually looked ridiculous. What was I doing here? What a waste! I was happier not knowing what a shallow doof I was head-over-heels for.

As another sappy slow song began, I felt a small tug on my sleeve.

"Are you all right Annie?" Patrick's kind voice permeated my fugue state.

"Oh, yes. Thank you, Patrick. I really am," I looked up at him.

Those are the darkest bluest eyes I have ever seen.

I never realized how tall he was before.

"Okay, you just looked upset," he turned as if to go.

Viva le Resistance!

"Patrick," he stopped and looked back at me, "Would you like to dance with me?"

He smiled.

We walked back out to the center of the dance floor hand-in-hand. Patrick and I swayed to the music. Occasionally, he would whisper something in my ear that would make me laugh. As the night wore on, I felt more comfortable in his arms. I leaned into him and rested my cheek on his chest.

He has a broad chest? When did THAT happen?

A few times the music picked up speed. We would walk off the dance floor and talk quietly together until another slow number was ready. Patrick, it turns out, was funny and insightful.

The evening was magical. As the last song was announced we again turned to hold each other.

"Annie!" I heard Sam shout.

What the?

"Annie, I did it. I told Julie there was no way it was going to happen between us. I told her Annie. I told her that I like you and only you. I'm sorry I kissed her Annie, I really am. We can still end this night together," he was out of breath at the end.

Everyone around us was staring with that I-shouldn't-look-but-I-can't-look-away sort of expression. Laurie clasped her hands together excitedly and took a little happy jump, with her eyebrows raised almost to her hairline.

She looked so pleased for me.

Sam had done it.

He had stood up for himself and us.

He risked the scorn of the bagmen and the cliquey's to share his true feelings about me. He reached out for my hand and looked expectantly at me. Patrick gave me an encouraging smile and quietly turned away.

Patrick started to walk back to the bleachers. My hand shot out and grasped his sleeve. He stopped, but didn't turn around.

Viva le Resistance!

Sam looked at my hand on Patrick's arm. He looked up at me with a questioning stare.

"Thank you Sam, but I am dancing with Patrick," I looked up, "If he still wants to, that is."

Patrick stared uncomprehendingly for a moment.

"I really do want that," he agreed, gently taking my hand in his.

Sam watched momentarily, and then lowering his head, he walked away.

Patrick held me close and whispered into my ear, "You know, don't you, that this is what I've hoped for since second grade."

Viva le Resistance!

Looking up inquisitively, I asked, "What do you mean?"

"Do you remember when we played at recess? You were the mother and I was your decoration," he continued, "I fell for you then and always imagined that some day…"

He left the comment hanging.

I can't believe he remembers that.

Patrick leaned back in holding me close. It felt somehow 'right' to be held by him. The music, the lights, the people dancing on either side of us, it was wonderful!

267

Viva le Resistance!

"Viva le Resistance!" Cara cried
dancing merrily by.

Viva le Resistance!

WE HOPE YOU HAVE ENJOYED VIVA LE
RESISTANCE! FOR MORE ANNIE
BOOKS, PLEASE VISIT:

www.anniebooks.com

-Michelle and Josh\

Viva le Resistance!

Author: Michelle Fattig, Ed.S.
Michelle is a school psychologist and medical technologist, who volunteers as a parent advocate, and provides professional development to parents and educators, regarding Individuals with Disabilites Education Act (IDEA), Improving Learning for Children with Disabilities (ILCD), Hidden Disabilites, and Response to Intervention (RTI). She is a proud veteran of the Air Force and previous school board member. Michelle has Asperger's Syndrome, Attention Deficit with Hyperactivity Disorder, and learning disabilities. She is a doctoral candidate in Education Leadership. In her 'spare time,' she enjoys spending time with her family.

Illustrator: Josh is a junior in high school, and is incredibly gifted in art and music. Josh has many other wonderful attributes, and he also has the joy of Asperger's Syndrome, Attention Deficit Disorder (he firmly believes that having one less letter in his disorder makes him LESS disabled than his mom), and learning disabilities. Josh enjoys music, very much, he enjoys LESS much, illustrating for his mother. He, however, being the dutiful son, perseveres!

Viva le Resistance!

Model, editor, overall critique'er: Lili is a second grade student, and budding attorney. She will be overseeing and generally directing any and all activities of the above mentioned employees.